The Bible Answer Man:
Walter Martin
and Hank Hanegraaff

Dr. Martin's Daughter Reflects on CRI's Founder, Its History, and Its Current President

Cindee Martin Morgan

Copyright © 2019 Walter Martin Jude 3

All rights reserved.

ISBN: 9781079977882

Cindee Martin Morgan has written an insightful historical work summarizing the life and ministry of her father, Walter R. Martin. Walter has been widely acclaimed as the father of the cult and countercult movement. He was the founder of a highly influential countercult ministry, the Christian Research Institute, which eventually spawned the popular *Bible Answer Man* broadcast program.

Cindee Martin Morgan provides an insider's view of the struggles and victories in both the Martin family and his international ministry. In the process, she explains many of the successes and controversies associated with CRI. Prominently presented within is Walter's friendship and ministerial relationship with his personally appointed successor Hank Hanegraaff. Hanegraaff's controversial conversion to Eastern Orthodoxy is presented in much detail in the later chapters. Given the significance of this ministry and of these men, Cindee's book should be of great interest to those who are interested in Christianity in America today.

Kenneth L. Gentry, Jr., ThD
Director of GoodBirth Ministries

As a colleague of Walter Martin in the 1970s, I came to greatly admire his extraordinary mind and his staunch commitment to defending biblical truth. Little did I know that, years later, a mutual friend and colleague, Hank Hanegraaff, would assume the reins to take the Christian Research Institute to an entirely new level of influence and global impact. For those interested in an up-close-and-personal, behind-the-scenes look at the trials, tribulations, and triumphs of one of the world's premier apologetics ministries, *The Bible Answer Man* by Walter Martin's daughter Cindee provides fascinating insights into a remarkable history of two men committed to transforming the world with the truths of God's Word.

Larry F. Johnston
President of McConkey/Johnston International

I can't recommend highly enough Cindee Martin Morgan's new book *The Bible Answer Man: Walter Martin and Hank Hanegraaff — Dr. Martin's Daughter Reflects on CRI's Founder, Its History, and Its Current President*. This wonderful read breaks down the life of two amazing men of God and gives you a behind-the-scenes look at how God used these two men in a powerful way to build the Christian Research Institute (CRI) into one of the most impactful and Kingdom-furthering Christian ministries the world has ever known. Cindee Martin Morgan, the daughter of Walter Martin, gives her firsthand account of how these two men changed her life, and have helped to change the life of millions for good. Her writing is beautiful and winsome, and her storytelling gift makes it feel like you're a firsthand witness. Read *The Bible Answer Man* as soon as you can!

Matt Barber
Cofounder and General Counsel of Christian Civil Rights Watch (CCRW)

Cindee Martin Morgan, in this manuscript, provides an important historical account of the ministry and history of her father, Walter R. Martin, and the Christian Research Institute. For those of us who came of age in the 1970s and 1980s, Martin and CRI were formative influences in our development as Christians.

Francis J. Beckwith
Professor of Philosophy and Church–State Studies (Department of Philosophy),
Associate Director of Graduate Studies (Department of Philosophy),
Baylor University

I have been a friend of the Martin family since my childhood. My father, Walter Bjorck Jr., was a good friend of Walter Martin. He was part of the Christian Research Institute staff and the *Bible Answer Man* program when it first came on the church scene. I am very happy to see this book published. I believe Walter Martin and my father would be happy to see it as well. Cindee Martin Morgan's book *The Bible Answer Man* successfully demonstrates how the phrase C. S. Lewis used, "mere Christianity," applies to all phases of the ministry of CRI as it continues to endeavor to aid the whole body of Christ. I wish great success for this interesting and well-written book and the whole ongoing ministry of CRI.

Walter Bjorck Jr.

Cindee Martin Morgan gives a fascinating account of her father — Walter Martin — and the birth of the Christian Research Institute (CRI). This work propels the reader back in time, revealing what it was like to be raised by the father of the countercult movement painted across the backdrop of Walter Martin's riveting interactions with famous figures. Cindee lays out an intriguing timeline that illuminates the sovereignty of God, in all things, and how the Lord positioned Hank Hanegraaff to take the reins of this apologetic ministry when God called its founder home in 1989. Both these incredible men have impacted my life in profound ways, giving me the theological groundwork for my prolife work. This book is sure to bless those, like me, who have been helped by CRI — a ministry that has endured for more than half a century.

Troy Newman
President of Operation Rescue
Cofounder of the Center for Medical Progress (CMP)

I cannot emphasize enough how the teachings of Dr. Walter Martin impacted my Christian life. His book *The Kingdom of the Cults* transformed my life and gave me a love and a passion to witness to Mormons and Jehovah's Witnesses. Cindee does a masterful job in this powerful memoir of chronicling the life of her father and his dedication to defending God's truth, with the establishment of the Christian Research Institute. I was very impressed by the delicate way she handled Hank Hanegraaff's decision to become a member of the Orthodox Church. True to the spirit of her father, she pointed out that we must never compromise the essentials of the faith and must treat our brothers with love and respect if we disagree with their doctrinal positions. This book is a must read if you were challenged by the books of Dr. Martin and also impacted by the *Bible Answer Man* broadcast. A great job, Cindee!

Randy Noble
Christian Author
Host of the Radio Program, *The Cross in the Desert: Speaking Hope and Freedom to Iran*

First Peter 3:15 epitomized the ministry of the late theologian and biblical scholar and founder of the Christian Research Institute, Dr. Walter Martin. This verse continues to be the focus of Hank Hanegraaff, current president of CRI and radio host of the *Bible Answer Man* broadcast. I've had the privilege down through the years to be exposed to the brilliant mind and scholarship of Dr. Walter Martin, through his preaching, teaching, and Christian apologetics ministry, during my undergraduate studies while in Bible college. After reading the masterpiece *Kingdom of the Cults* in the late '80s, I knew I wanted my focus to also be in Christian apologetics.

Reading *The Bible Answer Man*, I understand in ways that I never did before as to why Walter Martin was so passionate and zealous in his defense of the gospel. I had heard him on the radio, and even saw him a few times on shows like the *John Ankerberg Show*, but when one reads this book by his precious daughter Cindee, you realize that you really didn't know him or his heartbeat for his family and ministry very well. Cindee, as only a daughter could, takes us into the privacy of her father's mind and heart, and allows us to peer into his soul and see what made him the man that he became. I became significantly more appreciative of Dr. Martin's love for his Lord and for the work that God called him to do.

The reader will especially appreciate Cindee's honesty in having to divulge some of the painful experiences of her family and the ministry of CRI. However, rather than being repelled by such personal human experiences, I believe they will be drawn in to see how this family of faith overcame the breakup of a marriage, the healing of sickness and disease, the reconciliation of broken relationships, and how God has used their pain to glorify His name and strengthen them in the process. Thank you, Cindee, for allowing God to use your hurts and painful experiences to make, mold, and prepare you for writing this amazing book. I strongly recommend that every Christian that has ever heard Dr. Walter Martin's messages, pick up a copy…and perhaps buy a second copy to give to a loved one or a friend. I promise you will not be able to put the book down, because every word will capture your heart and imagination.

Hank Hanegraaff has been used of God in a myriad of ways to bless the Body of Christ. After I became acquainted with him through the radio ministry of the *Bible Answer Man*, I made it a point to listen to him daily to see how he handled the caller's various questions. I was always impressed with Hank's knowledge of the Word, but more significantly, I was struck by his genuine concern and gentleness toward each caller. He has always exhibited a sincere sense of grace and love toward those who simply did not understand biblical truth, and even while many wanted to take him to task in an abrasive and unkind manner, Hank always sought to exemplify Christ in his demeanor and tone. I admire his determination to continue the strong work of defending the Christian faith, given what he has gone through in terms of his physical challenges as well as the attacks on his uniting with the Greek Orthodox Church.

Hank's great book Christianity in Crisis further cemented my choice to go into the Christian apologetics field, as when it was written, I was dealing with many of the false teachings in a sermon series and found the material very helpful. There can be no question that God has used both Dr. Walter Martin and Hank Hanegraaff in the building of his Kingdom through the ministry of CRI and BAM. This book brilliantly brings two wonderful godly men's journeys into full view and shows how God navigated the circumstances that brought them together for the divine purpose of equipping believers to defend the faith that was once and for all delivered unto the saints!

Wayne C. Cooper
Pastor, Teacher
Lincoln Avenue Christian Church
Pasadena, California

In this endearing personal memoir, Cindee, daughter of the late Walter Martin (probably best known for his book *The Kingdom of the Cults*), adds clarity — and in some needed instances, correction — to questions connected with the Christian Research Institute, a prominent conservative evangelical countercult and apologetics ministry that Martin founded in 1960. Following Martin's death in 1989, the leadership of CRI was succeeded by Hank Hanegraaff, the famed *Bible Answer Man*, whose conversion to Eastern Orthodoxy in 2017 caused a stir among some within Evangelicalism who would do well to read the perspective Cindee brings. Readers of this chronicle will not only enjoy the many enlightening behind-the-scenes glimpses into the lives of these two great men but also gain from rare firsthand interviews and anecdotes valuable insight into how God does indeed move in a mysterious (and sometimes amusing) way his wonders to perform.

Rolley Haggard
Abortion Abolitionist
Former Feature Writer for *Breakpoint*

The Bible Answer Man
Walter Martin and Hank Hanegraaff

In loving memory of my father, Walter Martin, who taught me to "turn my eyes upon Jesus," to trust Him, and to seek His face.

To my dear husband Rick, whose faithfulness to the gospel gives me greater courage to march on the battlefield the children of God must live on.

CONTENTS

	Acknowledgments	i
1	Defending an Eternal Truth in a Supernatural Courtroom	1
2	The Martin Family	13
3	New Beginnings: CRI on the World Stage	25
4	Working for CRI, Meeting Hal Lindsey, and Dispensationalism	32
5	More Heirloom Memories, Madalyn Murray O'Hair, the Osmond Brothers, and *The Kingdom of the Cults*	56
6	Catholicism, John Ankerberg, and the Trinity Broadcasting Network (TBN)	63
7	Final Days and Witnessing to Muhammad Ali	74
8	"It was sea and islands now. The great continent had sunk like Atlantis."	81
9	For the Sake of Truth	92
10	A Theological Blast from the Past: The Local Church and CRI	101
11	Walter Martin's Views	106
12	Dr. John Warwick Montgomery	110
13	Hank Hanegraaff and the Greek Orthodox Church	122
14	Called to Suffer	131

Appendix	Hank Hanegraaff: An In-Depth Interview	135
	Selected Biography	174
	About the Author	175

PREFACE

This book, while containing relevant biographical information, is *not* a biography of Walter Martin. It highlights the ministry God raised up through Walter Martin almost six decades ago, the Christian Research Institute (CRI), and unpacks some of its triumphs and trials. It is a daughter's reflections on seasons of her father's life — both public and private — and is, in a limited sense, a memoir. It answers many questions, such as: *What was it like to have Walter Martin as a father?* (The question I am asked most frequently.) *Was Walter Martin a dispensationalist, like his friend Hal Lindsey? Why was Walter Martin not invited back on the Trinity Broadcasting Network? What happened, behind the scenes when he debated America's most infamous atheist, Madalyn Murray O'Hair? Why didn't he believe the Catholic Church is a cult? What happened, off camera, when Walter Martin debated Fr. Mitch Pacwa on The John Ankerberg Show? Would my father agree with CRI's current assessment of the "Local Church" Movement of Watchman Nee and Witness Lee? How did God give Walter Martin the opportunity to witness to Muhammed Ali and Phil Donahue face-to-face? When did Anderson Cooper's mother help the Martin family? How did the Lord make a way for the Osmond brothers to hear Walter Martin preach about Mormonism? Did my father believe the gift of healing is for today?* Many Walter Martin tributes from well-known leaders are also included.

This book is also an honest look at CRI's president, Hank Hanegraaff, and the controversy that shook the Evangelical world when he joined the Greek Orthodox Church. Do his beliefs conflict with the gospel handed down through the ages? Would Walter Martin have viewed him as an apostate? A look at what Walter Martin, Martin Luther, J. C. Ryle, J. I. Packer, and C. S. Lewis believed might give you serious pause as to how to answer this important question. In addition, this book includes an in-depth interview with Hank Hanegraaff, the president of the Christian Research Institute. Hank discusses his faith, his family, CRI, and his friendship with Walter Martin — including rarely heard details about the moments after Hank learned of his death — and his friendship with R. C. Sproul and others.

I have known few people, on a personal level, who have had the kind of calling, excitement, passion, and stamina my father had when it came to accomplishing the goals the Lord set before him. My grandparents urged my father to study law like his father, George Washington Martin II, a well-known New York county court judge back in the days of Al Capone. My grandfather earned his law degree from Yale University. He had a rather colorful career and resided over cases that involved underworld figures. Many of those cases were reported in the *New York Times*. His son — and the youngest child of seven — would decide, however, that this would not be the backdrop of *his* life. When God saved Walter Martin, he set his feet on a different path, calling him to defend an eternal truth and justice in a supernatural courtroom. Walter Martin's life calling would be to publicly preach, teach, and defend the gospel of Jesus Christ.

To say the Lord gave Walter Martin wisdom and foresight — more than thirty years ago — to protect CRI, in the event of his death, is an understatement. When I learned the steps he had taken, I became *even more proud of him* — something I didn't believe was possible. Walter Martin followed the Lord's leading to seek out and personally vet a young dynamic leader that God would use to keep CRI from dying with its founder. He was painfully aware that most ministries usually do not survive after a ministry leader's death.

I first met Hank Hanegraaff at a Claim Jumper restaurant in Mission Viejo, California, when my father and I bumped into him having lunch there. My dad introduced me to Hank and indicated that the Lord had brought him to the Christian Research Institute. I remember, later that year, seeing Hank at my father's home and meeting his wife, Kathy. Although my husband Rick and I lived in Arizona at the time, we often visited my dad. It was evident that Hank Hanegraaff and Walter Martin were excited about what the Lord was doing at CRI. Years later, I learned that during this final chapter of my father's life, he *repeatedly* had asked his large Sunday school class to pray for Hank and the new leadership position Hank was considering accepting at CRI. In April of 1989 — two months prior to his death — Walter Martin introduced Hank to his class as his "friend" and the new "executive vice president of CRI."

To this day, the ship of CRI continues to sail choppy theological seas three decades after the death of its founder. This did not happen by chance; it happened by design. Only the Lord knows how many lives have been blessed — how many souls have been saved — because of this apologetic ministry the Lord raised up over a half century ago. By the providence of God, Walter Martin accomplished everything he set out to accomplish reminding me of the Scripture, "He who has begun a good work in you will complete it." (Philippians 1:6)[1]

---

[1] All Bible quotations that are not quoted in dialogue are from the New King James Version unless otherwise indicated.

1

DEFENDING AN ETERNAL TRUTH IN A SUPERNATURAL COURTROOM

"Beloved, while I was very diligent to write to you concerning our common salvation, I found it necessary to write to you exhorting you to contend earnestly for the faith which was once for all delivered to the saints."
(Jude 3)

I have always found it intriguing that my father's mother was Roman Catholic, and his father was Episcopalian. Apparently, my father inherited his thick skin from his parents, not overly concerned if either camp had their feathers ruffled. Throughout his life, my grandfather maintained close friendships with his Catholic friends in his community. My father was born in Brooklyn, New York, one year before the Great Depression. It was a delight to receive this newspaper clipping from my dear cousin Susan, who loved her Uncle Walt. A newspaper of the day reported:

> Judge George W. Martin's absence from the Brooklyn County court bench for two days last week has been explained. It wasn't a case of sickness, but a case of happiness. For a baby boy was added to the Martin household. The youngster, who is the Martins' seventh child, arrived a week ago yesterday at Flower hospital, Manhattan, where both mother and child were reported yesterday as doing nicely. One of the reasons given for the judge's absence was that he was afraid

his happiness would cause him to lose his judicial dignity.[1]

This is the most charming birth announcement I've ever read. It is fascinating to have the opportunity to read my grandfather's own words at the time of my father's birth. I never had the opportunity to know him; he died before I was born. It is heartwarming to gain a glimpse of the joy he felt when his youngest son came into the world.

My dad mentioned how the Lord mercifully had spared his family severe hardship during the Great Depression, this dark time in world history when breadlines and soup kitchens were the norm. He was named Walter after one of the world's most prominent surgeons in New York, Walter Gray Crump, who was also the Martin family's doctor. Walter Martin was given his middle name, Ralston, after the New York City Water Commissioner Harry Ralston. Both men were close friends of his father. My dad publicly shared (in response to questions during his Bible class) what he thought of the names he was given at birth. Unpacked in a humorous way, he confessed, "I'm glad they left the *Martin* in there, because they already had two alien names." My grandfather had his youngest son baptized in the Episcopal Church but sent him to Catholic schools for his elementary education. I recall my dad mentioning the nuns in his school. Knowing how strict they were, I chuckle at the thought of the future *Bible Answer Man* misbehaving on their watch. Walter Martin later attended Stony Brook School. He was baptized for the second time in the Hegemen Chapel as a young adult. Dr. Frank Gaebelein, Stony Brook's headmaster, became my father's first spiritual mentor. Gaebelein was a highly respected author and editor who served the Lord at Stony Brook for forty years. He and Walter Martin became lifelong friends.

I had the distinct honor of meeting the distinguished Dr. Gaebelein in 1981. A photo of him was displayed on a wall in my father's house and was later gifted to me. I spent time with this unforgettable brother in Christ at our home in San Juan, California. He came for an extended visit following the death of his dear wife, Dorothy. We took walks together and talked about the Lord and his former student Walter Martin. He was quite proud of him — the kind of pride a father shows in a son. I will never forget how he was kind enough to patiently sit in our living room with me and edit a Christian poem I'd written. He graciously encouraged me as a writer; I was only twenty years old at the time. Dr. Gaebelein celebrated my dad's fifty-third birthday with us and gave him a NIV Zondervan Bible bearing this simple inscription:

For Walter Martin, my friend and brother in the Lord, who is using

---

[1] "Happiness Kept Him off the Bench," *Daily News*, September 16, 1928, p. 134; available at https://www.newspapers.com.

Scripture so effectively in proclaiming and defending the gospel of Christ.
—Frank Gaebelein Phil. 4:19, September 10, 1981

As a freshman at Shelton College, New York, Walter Martin was already speaking on the cults — to anyone who would listen — and self-publishing small pamphlets to help lead people out of the darkness and into the light. I was deeply moved that my father would at times skip lunch hour to stand on the corner of Wall Street and Broadway to engage with people and to answer questions about Christianity and the Word of God — a bit of a "street evangelist." Walter Martin demonstrated a tremendous love for Christ and for the lost. Without question, this type of outreach takes courage; he was never in short supply of it. In 1951, he became an ordained Baptist minister.

During Walter Martin's college days, he met my lovely mom, Elaine Jacobson, who was a Shelton college student herself and an aspiring model. They became friends, and she typed his papers. I remember her telling me, with a grin, she only charged my dad a nickel a page. My father soon fell head over heels in love with his typist. Walter Martin's best friend, Anthony Collarile, also attended Shelton College. The three of them became inseparable. He eventually would work side by side with my father in ministry. I have fond childhood memories of this kindhearted man, "Uncle Tony," bringing me and my siblings birthday gifts and gold foiled chocolate "coins" when he visited. He enjoyed telling me how he remembered me in my highchair. When I was older, he was kind enough to give me violin lessons. As an adult, I was amazed to learn that Anthony Collarile was an accomplished musician who had played the violin with the West Chester Symphony Orchestra. Naturally, as a child, I didn't understand his accomplishments, nor did I possess an ounce of talent to play this instrument. Nonetheless, the lessons were an experience, as was hearing Uncle Tony serenade us with his violin.

After a short courtship, my parents were married in June of 1952 at the Oakwood Avenue Baptist Church in Arlington, New Jersey. Having practically no money to call their own, my mother wore a borrowed wedding dress. *The Nutley Sun* stated, "Miss Elaine Lois Jacobson, daughter of Rev. and Mrs. Joseph Murphy of 682 Bloomfield Avenue, became the bride June 14 of Rev. Walter R. Martin, son of Mrs. George R. Martin of Garden City, L.I., and the late Judge Martin....The bride is attending Shelton College, New York. An alumnus of Shelton, Mr. Martin is a student at New York University."[2]

My parent's first modest home was my grandmother's attic. During the following year, Walter Martin briefly became a teacher at Shelton College and

---

[2] *The Nutley Sun,* June 27, 1952.

cowrote his first book, *Jehovah of the Watchtower*, with Norman Klann. This book identifies this cult and accurately explains its inner workings as it teaches the Christian church to recognize that Jehovah's Witnesses have completely distorted the gospel. *Jehovah of the Watchtower* equips the body of Christ to be able to witness to those ensnared in aberrant theology. It also was written as an outreach to those embedded in the darkness of this false religion. In the dedication of this book, Walter Martin writes, "To Jehovah's Witnesses everywhere who need to know the truth and the way to Him who alone is the life, Jesus Christ our Lord." Dr. Gaebelein wrote the Foreword. His words highlight how much the body of Christ needed this wake-up call and resource. "The church owes a debt of gratitude to Professor Walter R. Martin and the Reverend Norman Klann, who have collaborated in this authoritative study. In it, they have done a piece of pioneer research, and they have done it with scholarly competence and logical force. Eschewing hearsay evidence regarding Jehovah's Witnesses, they have gone to the sources, including the headquarters of the cult itself. The result is, so far as I know, the *first full-length portrait and analysis* of the movement to be published."[3] Indeed, this was a groundbreaking book. Several Walter Martin books, articles, and pamphlets soon followed that dealt with other cults and basic Christian doctrine.

To earn extra money, my father was a guest pastor for CBS's show *Bride and Groom*. He was delighted to marry his soon-to-be brother-in-law Everett Jacobson (and future longtime CRI board member) to my mom's best friend, Gladys Lubbert, during one of the shows.

It was fun to see my parents, aunt, and uncle in this charming blast from the past that captures them in a surreal moment in time. Watching the ceremony makes me feel like I'm seeing an old Hollywood love story. I recall my grandmother, decades later, mentioning the generous gifts CBS lavished on the couples that appeared on *Bride and Groom*. A charming historical clip of the wedding can be seen on our WalterMartinJude3 YouTube channel.[4] This clip is a glimpse of America's marriage values before many in our country abandoned God's design for it. I am proud of Walter Martin for boldly upholding the Word of God. He never wavered on this issue, as many in the church have done.

A larger-than-life figure the Lord used in my father's life at this time was

---

[3] From the Foreword in *Jehovah of the Watchtower*, rev. ed. (Chicago: Moody Press, 1974), emphasis in original.
[4] WalterMartinJude3, "Dr. Walter Martin – *Bride and Groom* show – CBS, 1953," YouTube video, 9:54, February 14, 2010, https://www.youtube.com/watch?v=lqfUWIpe_m0.

the late Dr. Donald Grey Barnhouse.[5] He, too, mentored Walter Martin. As Barnhouse's protégé, Walter Martin classified himself as a Baptist, yet he highly esteemed this theological giant who was a Reformed Presbyterian Pastor (RPC). The two men forged a friendship the Lord used to help equip Walter Martin to one day found his own ministry. Donald Barnhouse was a much-loved Presbyterian pastor, theologian, radio pioneer, and prolific writer who began the radio ministry *Dr. Barnhouse and The Bible*.[6] You can tune in, to this day, and hear this charismatic former pastor of the Tenth Presbyterian Church. Former US Surgeon General C. Everett Koop attended Barnhouse's church for more than twenty years. He had high regard for his pastor, once stating, "His authoritative voice held my attention, his physical appearance was arresting, and his preaching was teaching of the highest intellectual order....I always marveled at the simplicity of the faith of this very intelligent and learned man."[7]

Barnhouse was the founding editor of the monthly periodical *Eternity* magazine. He invited Walter Martin to be a columnist. Walter Martin served as a regular contributing editor and also became a cohost of Barnhouse's *Bible Study Hour*. It was clear the Lord was also setting the stage for Walter Martin's own radio ministry. God was paving the way for my father to reach a wider audience — a theological Paul Revere warning the church of the danger the cults presented to the body of Christ.

God's calling on Walter Martin's life took root long before leaving his twenties. He was focused and driven by what the Lord had purposed for him to do. He founded the division of Cult Apologetics at Zondervan Publishing House. He published two more books, one of which was *The Rise of the Cults*, a summary guide to the major cults.[8] Among the many gifts God had given him was a photographic memory; I recall him telling me he had read a dictionary in order to retain more knowledge of words and their definitions. He had an extraordinary ability to store information mentally. At the age of twenty-eight, he obtained a master's degree from New York University and Biblical Seminary.

During the whirlwind of ministry my parents were caught up in, they earnestly prayed for children. After a few years of longing for them, my

---

[5] "Donald Barnhouse," Wikipedia, https://en.wikipedia.org/wiki/Donald_Barnhouse.
[6] *Dr. Barnhouse and the Bible*, Alliance of Confessing Evangelicals, www.alliancenet.org/dr-barnhouse-the-bible.
[7] *Dr. Barnhouse and the Bible*, Alliance of Confessing Evangelicals, www.alliancenet.org/dr-barnhouse-the-bible.
[8] "A Brief Chronology of Walter R. Martin's Ministry," *Christian Research Newsletter* 2, no. 4 (1989), 4.

mother was told she needed a surgery to correct a simple issue that was not allowing her to conceive. They were overjoyed when the surgery was successful. My parents had their first son, Bryan, who was soon followed by my sister, Jill. The Lord had answered their prayers.

Between the years of 1956 and 1957, Walter Martin and Donald Barnhouse engaged in a formal conference with several major representatives of the General Conference of Seventh-day Adventism. The purpose of this meeting was to gather doctrinal information on this controversial group. The Adventist denomination published *Questions on Doctrine* primarily in response to Walter Martin's theological concerns. Walter Martin and Donald Barnhouse wrote a number of important articles on Seventh-day Adventism for *Eternity* magazine.[9] Barnhouse received extreme criticism for his article "Are the Seventh-Day Adventists Christians?" In his wife Margaret's biography of her husband, *The Man Barnhouse*, she writes, "The reaction was immediate: outraged canceling of subscriptions or grateful commendation because [he] had the courage to…admit he had been wrong in the past about the Adventists."[10] Barnhouse suffered the backlash of standing by his conscience before the Lord. Both Barnhouse and Walter Martin publicly concluded and argued that Seventh-day Adventists were indeed brothers and sisters in Christ who held to the essential basic doctrines of Christianity, with certain heterodox teachings.

After the birth of his second son, Daniel, Walter Martin published *The Truth about Seventh-day Adventism* in 1960. Neither Dr. Barnhouse nor Walter Martin missed an opportunity to proclaim the truth, no matter what the cost. Without question, the Lord used the close relationship my father had with Dr. Barnhouse to plant his feet on the theological grid, enabling him to point millions of spiritually dead people to the Rock of Ages and, with God's help, free lost souls from the shifting sands of false doctrines.

Walter Martin taught at Kings College for five years. On October 1, 1960, he founded The Christian Research Institute (CRI) — the same year I was conceived. The vision for CRI had long been in the works in Walter Martin's mind, and now it had become a reality, by the providence of God. An Evangelical countercult apologetics ministry was born.

The 1960s ushered in the hippie counterculture in America. During this era, Walter Martin traveled frequently with Billy Graham and World Vision founder Bob Pierce, addressing thousands in open-air church meetings about

---

[9] "A Brief Chronology of Walter R. Martin's Ministry," *Christian Research Newsletter* 2, no. 4 (1989), 4.

[10] Margaret N. Barnhouse, *That Man Barnhouse* (Wheaton, IL: https://www.revolvy.com/page/Donald-Barnhouse?cr=1, 1983).

the theological problems posed by the cults.[11] My parents brought us to Billy Graham crusades. They were excited to have an inspiring friendship with the Rev. Billy Graham and his wife, Ruth. They looked up to this iconic couple. They were thrilled to see the Lord using Rev. Graham to reach millions of people needing to hear the good news of the gospel. I remember my mother telling me how she and Ruth discussed the hardships of their husbands having to travel so much for ministry. She liked Ruth very much. My brother Danny was excited to later have the opportunity to room with Billy Graham's son, Ned, at Stony Brook. It is a sort of heart keepsake of mine to recall what Rev. Billy Graham once said of my father. He stated that he was "one of the most articulate spokesmen for evangelical Christianity that I know."[12] I formally accepted Christ as my Savior while watching a Billy Graham Crusade on television at the age of nine. While I can't remember a time in my life that I didn't love Jesus, I recall this was the moment I better understood that hell is real and that I needed a Savior. Billy Graham put the fear of God in me.

Having traveled extensively, Walter Martin was part of the Pastor's Conference Team of World Vision Inc. He traveled roughly 25,000 miles and spoke to over 5,000 Christians about the problem of non-Christian cults on the mission field."[13]

When I was one year old, my parents moved our family to Oakland, a small town in New Jersey. I was surprised to learn that my father held Bible studies in former actress Gloria Vanderbilt's home. (Gloria was the mother of CNN's news anchor Anderson Cooper.) My mother mentioned to me how Gloria graciously had loaned my parents the down payment to buy the house they purchased on what became our much-loved street, Eagle Crest Place.

Walter Martin's book, dealing with the cult of Mormonism, was published shortly after our move to Oakland in 1962. *The Maze of Mormonism* is a handbook on Mormon history and theology for Christian workers. Walter Bjorck Jr., a close friend of my father's, was a gifted graphic artist (and CRI researcher) who did the artwork for this extraordinary book. The Lord surrounded my father with talented people with a deep love for Jesus Christ

---

[11] "Walter Ralston Martin," Wikipedia, https://en.wikipedia.org/wiki/Walter_Ralston_Martin.

[12] Allison Samuels, "'The Bible Answer Man' Even Had a Posthumous Solution," *The Los Angeles Times*, October 9, 1989, http://articles.latimes.com/1989-10-09/local/me-210_1_bible-answer-man.

[13] "A Brief Chronology of Walter R. Martin's Ministry," *Christian Research Newsletter* 2, no. 4 (1989), 4.

and a desire to see the gospel preached to every tribe and nation.

On a side note, my husband Rick and I had the opportunity one summer to witness to several Mormon missionaries. My father's resources helped equip us to put our best theological foot forward. Two young Mormon missionaries had biked to our home, wanting to witness to us, and we invited them inside. We opened our Bibles, and they opened their Book of Mormon. As Walter Martin pointed out on many occasions, this book is a plagiarism of the King James Bible that has been renamed The Book of Mormon. He often said you could get saved reading it. So, in a sense, we found our common ground with these missionaries and dug in. Step by step, we laid out for them how the Mormon Church redefines Christian terms, and we contrasted their meanings with the truth. We sought to help them understand that their Jesus is *not* the Jesus of the Bible. The Jesus of Mormonism is the god of *this* world only. The Bible says that Jesus is the *only* God — the second person of the Trinity. They especially struggled with the concept of the Trinity, but they listened intently. We biblically demonstrated that Jesus is *not* the spirit brother of Lucifer. The *real* Jesus is not related to Lucifer.

We kept inviting them back, and they kept coming. Sometimes a new missionary would replace one who had finished his mission. We prayed together and used a tip my father gave to those trying to witness to the cults. He said if they are willing to pray with you, use this unique opportunity to share the gospel with them during your prayer, in addition to discussions with them.

Rick and I grew to care for these Mormons, and a number of times we had them over for dinner. We targeted the Mormon doctrine that teaches that Mormon men can become gods of their own planets, have multiple wives, and procreate throughout eternity if they are good enough and rise to a high enough level in the Church. Our respectful exchanges seemed to resonate with one of the Mormon missionaries in particular. When the summer ended and they said their goodbyes, he gave us his Book of Mormon. We gave him a tape of contemporary hymns packed with the gospel and the true identity of Jesus Christ. We were thankful the Lord had graciously given us many opportunities to plant seeds. I thank God he began using my father to warn the church, and those deceived by Mormonism, about a dangerous doctrine that appears holy on the surface but is spiritually fatal to its core.

Walter Martin launched *Dateline Eternity* in 1963 — his *first* radio program. He also conceived of the brilliant idea of creating a computer data bank of apologetics information. The concept was eventually packaged under the acronym SENT/EAST (Electronic Answering Search Technology).[14] In

---

[14] "Christian Research Institute," Wikipedia, https://en.wikipedia.org/wiki/Christian_Research_Institute.

1968, a symposium of scholars was convened in Austria, where the plans for CRI's computerized apologetics data bank were presented in lectures by my father and his close friend John Warwick Montgomery.[15] Many of these details were reported in *Christianity Today* and then in Montgomery's book *Computers, Cultural Change, and the Christ*.[16] Walter Martin's idea was to create a database of information for the body of Christ and for the lost, to enable them to find answers at their fingertips. Decades later, he told me he hoped to have a system like this in place to assist him, in answering questions, when he did his radio program. My father's broad vision for CRI was clearly ahead of its time.

Walter Martin began appearing on NBC's *Long John Nebel Show* in 1964. Nebel was a popular all-night radio host with millions of regular listeners. My father was a regular panel guest appearing on this broadcast more than eighty times. He debated many non-Christians.[17] Walter Martin's 1968 spirited debate with America's most famous atheist, Madalyn Murray O'Hair, is one of his most notable. O'Hair's historic lawsuit resulting in the banning of the Bible and prayer in public schools made her an intimidating social force. The several hours of exchange between O'Hair, Martin, Nebel, his callers, and (briefly) a rabbi is riveting. It showcases the hatred O'Hair had for Christianity. She mocks, repeatedly interrupts, insults, name calls, and often laughs at Walter Martin as he steadfastly proclaims the gospel with conviction. Not surprisingly, O'Hair refers to Christianity as "rubbish" and accuses my father of being an anti-Semite for boldly stating that some of the Jews, back in the day of Christ, were responsible for His crucifixion. Without apology, my father spells out the truth, ignoring their objections to it:

> The New Testament record states that Jesus Christ died for the sins of the world as the Son of God. The Jews rejected Him as the Messiah and Gentiles after that accepted Him. Through the centuries Jews and Gentiles have disagreed on this basic point and Christians have received Him as the Messiah. I simply maintain that in the Old Testament God said the Jews were His chosen people and that they were the channel of salvation to the Gentiles. I maintain that the New Testament is the fulfillment of the Old Testament and

---

[15] "John Warwick Montgomery," Apologetics Academy, http://www.apologeticsacademy.eu/Professor_John_Warwick_Montgomery.php.

[16] "Christian Research Institute," Wikipedia, https://en.wikipedia.org/wiki/Christian_Research_Institute.

[17] "A Brief Chronology of Walter R. Martin's Ministry," *Christian Research Newsletter* 2, no. 4 (1989), 4.

that through Jesus Christ the Savior of the world Christianity has become the channel of redemption to the whole world including the Jew. And, any Jew and any Gentile who rejects Jesus Christ as Lord and Savior after God's love to them shown on the cross, is guilty of crucifying Him afresh. That's what the New Testament says, and I believe it.[18]

Walter Martin was falsely accused of anti-Semitism for sharing the gospel of Jesus Christ. O'Hair's anger steadily grew. Every one of her fallacious arguments fell apart as the debate moved along. By the end of it, she was spitting nails. My father demonstrated the patience of a saint, never wavering from the truth of God's Word. My mom, who sat through O'Hair's relentless rudeness to her husband, could not believe the nastiness. The gentleman he was, Walter Martin offered to give Madalyn Murray O'Hair a ride after the program ended. My father's dear friend Walter Bjorck Jr. — also a CRI researcher — who'd accompanied my parents that night said Madalyn got "very huffy," having no interest in taking them up on it. I have to smile when I think of my dad offering her a ride. I am certain he made the offer to try to have another opportunity to share Christ with this atheist who was on the highway to hell. Bjorck later remarked that O'Hair could not understand kindness from a Christian. While researching this book, I was thankful to have learned most of these scarcely known details firsthand from Walter Bjorck Jr.'s son — my friend — who is named after his father. (More on Madalyn later.)

By this time in CRI's history, my father's college friend, Anthony Collarile, had become an integral part of Walter Martin's ministry. Collarile (and others) contributed research data for *The Kingdom of the Cults* that has since become a classic. Walter Bjorck Jr. offered a number of manuscript suggestions, many of which were used by my father. This historic book was chosen by both *Christianity Today* and *Eternity* magazines as "one of the best" of the year in 1965.[19]

Dr. Martin defined what a cult is, in this work, by first quoting a liberal, Dr. Charles Braden, and then expanding on his definition. Braden explains, "…A cult, as I define it, is any religious group which differs significantly in one or more respects as to belief or practice from those religious groups

---

[18] Apologia Acts 17:17, "Walter Martin vs. Madalyn Murray O'Hair," YouTube video, 3:05:12, published April 22, 2012, https://www.youtube.com/watch?v=P4W0x959Jdc, accessed March 3, 2019.

[19] "A Brief Chronology of Walter R. Martin's Ministry," *Christian Research Newsletter* 2, no. 4 (1989), 4.

which are regarded as the normative expressions of religion in our total culture."[20]

Dr. Martin makes this important addition to Braden's words:

> I may add to this that a cult might also be defined as a group of people gathered about a specific person or person's misinterpretation of the Bible. For example, Jehovah's Witnesses are, for the most part, followers of the interpretations of Charles T. Russell and J. F. Rutherford… From a theological viewpoint, the cults contain many major deviations from historic Christianity. Yet paradoxically, they continue to insist that they are entitled to be classified as Christians….It has been wisely observed by someone that "a man who will not stand for something is quite likely to fall for almost anything." *So I have elected to stand on the ramparts of biblical Christianity as taught by the apostles, defended by the church fathers, rediscovered by the Reformers, and embodied in what is sometimes called Reformed theology.*[21]

This comprehensive theological cult digest continues to be used as a textbook in many colleges today and remains a valuable ministry tool for the body of Christ. It is a compelling example of how the work the Lord does, through each of His children, lives on even after we are home in heaven. A profound statement in *The Kingdom of the Cults* stood out to me as we continue to live in a day and age where millions of people believe there are many roads to heaven. Walter Martin unapologetically declared:

> I must dissent from the view that "all roads that lead to God are good" and believe instead the words of our Lord, "I am the way, the truth and the life: no man cometh unto the Father, but by Me" (John 14:6). It should be carefully noted that Jesus did not say, "I am one of many equally good ways" or, "I am a better way than the others, I am an aspect of truth; I am a fragment of the life." Instead, His claim was absolute, and allegiance to Him, as the Saviour of the world, was to take precedence over all the claims of men and religions.[22]

CRI grew to be a trusted theological think tank overflowing with resources for the body of Christ. Walter Martin continued to help the church learn what a cult is and how to reach out to those trapped inside its walls — cultists can't

---

[20] Dr. Charles Braden, in *The Kingdom of the Cults*, 1965, Preface, xii.
[21] *The Kingdom of the Cults*, 11–12, emphasis added.
[22] *The Kingdom of the Cults*, 13.

see, hear, or understand the truth nor escape this theological cell without *the key to the door*: Jesus Christ. My father also was determined to help Christians better understand *why* they believed what they believed and wanted to equip them to defend the truth of the gospel to a lost world.

Walter Martin began the *Bible Answer Man* program in 1965 with the prayer of reaching as many people as possible with the good news of Jesus Christ; it became the radio outreach of CRI. It was recognized by the National Religious Broadcasters as "one of the most controversially stimulating programs in Christian radio!"[23] Walter Bjorck Jr. often filled in for Walter Martin daily, answering questions about the Bible and the cults. Having no formal theological training, Bjorck later went on to do the same type of program for almost ten years, calling his program *The Bible Question Air*.

Not allowing any theological grass to grow under his feet, Walter Martin had the honor of taking over Dr. Barnhouse's New York City Bible class for several years. My mother helped him with the music ministry side of things; she was a gifted pianist.

With a growing family and the demands of founding a new ministry, the Martin children were blessed with a wonderful part-time nanny to help hold down the Martin fort. Rebecca, affectionately called Becky, married a theologian, James Bjornstad. He became the director of research at the Christian Research Institute for five years. Our family loved this couple. Becky was also my Kindergarten teacher at the Holy Cross Lutheran Church and Nursery School in Mahwah, New Jersey. She was one of the kindest people I have ever known. Rebecca Bjornstad, now with the Lord, was a Christian schoolteacher for thirty-seven years. Right before her death, she authored the book *Thomas Jefferson: The Freedom of a Nation* (Crossbooks, 2010).

---

[23] "A Brief Chronology of Walter R. Martin's Ministry," *Christian Research Newsletter* 2, no. 4 (1989), 4.

2

THE MARTIN FAMILY

I recall being proud of my dad when my age was still in single digits. On occasion, my older brother Danny and I would stand alongside him when he shook hands with the members of our church following a sermon he had preached. Easter Sunday, every year, was especially memorable for my sisters and me because my dad insisted we have a new Easter dress, hat, and gloves. My dad explained that this was something his parents did for his sisters when they were growing up — sort of a Martin family tradition. My parents emphasized Christ above all else, but did allow the Easter bunny to visit our home. Early Sunday morning, we each received a colorful Easter basket filled with chocolate eggs and a hollow chocolate bunny. They made sure we understood that this was just for fun; we knew it was not the real meaning of Easter.

We loved our church — known then as Van Riper Ellis Memorial Church. One of the ushers always had a piece of hard candy in his pockets for the children who entered the sanctuary. I'll never forget, though, how uncomfortable I thought those pews were and how challenging it was to sit still. It seemed that every other Sunday Danny and I were spanked for goofing off. My oldest brother once received the shock of his life when from the pulpit, *in the middle of his sermon,* my father flatly remarked, "Bryan, please behave." It worked; I don't think he ever misbehaved in church again. I recall one Sunday, in particular, when we arrived home from church, and I heard my mom tell my father to "spank Cindee the hardest; she was the worst." This memory makes me laugh now, but when I was small, it struck fear in my heart; I had a healthy respect for my parents. Like most Christian parents in their time and before it, they firmly believed in the Scriptural admonition that to spare the rod was to spoil the child.

After church on Sunday, we sometimes had church friends over for lunch. Typically, when we did, our family would stop at the bakery on the way home and get a yellow cake with chocolate icing — a favorite at our house. I loved meals in our dining room. One memorable Sunday dinner that stands out is when one of our guests had something interesting to share with their pastor and his wife about one of my siblings. As fate would have it, that child had parked himself under the table during this particular exchange. To his horror, he heard one of our guests inform our dad that his youngest son Danny had been coloring *on the church walls*. I am certain Danny didn't sit down easily for a while after that revelation in the Martin dining room. Needless to say, pastors' children are no different than the children in their congregations.

I didn't realize until I was grown the profound influence a godly father could have on a child's life. I recall lining my dolls up on the wall of our bathroom tub, pulling out the hamper and standing behind it, opening my Bible, and preaching a short message to my "congregation" (who doubled as my children), even shaking their hands after the service ended. I also saw to it my dolls were scolded should they misbehave and didn't hesitate to do it while I was behind my pulpit, either. Already the Lord was training me to be a good parent because of the faithfulness of my own. I remember one evening, in particular, trying to leave an amusement park — after a long day of rides, hotdogs, and cotton candy — and holding my sticky hands straight up in the air, begging my father to carry me. To my relief, he did. I laid my head on his shoulder feeling safe and loved. I also was a bit in shock, because due to his bad back, my father seldom carried his children once we were no longer toddlers. I knew this was a rare exception, and I was thankful. I believe my father's love, and the trust I had in him, helped set the stage for me to trust in the Lord and to one day recognize *His* love for me as well. I came to understand my Heavenly Father carries me when I am weary, and to rest in Him.

Another formative time with my father was as a first grader struggling with a prolonged illness. I could barely eat or keep anything down, was steadily dropping in weight, and I heard my dad ask the Lord to heal me; I was so ill the doctor made house calls. The last time he came, I heard him stress to my parents that I would need to be hospitalized "by morning" if my high fever didn't break. After the doctor left, my father scooped me up in his arms and held me a long time, before putting me to bed that night. The next morning, my fever broke. Looking back, it is evident to me that the love of Christian parents is the foundation the Lord laid in my life to help teach me to one day *lean* on *the everlasting arms*, and that no matter how dark the night, morning will come.

My father firmly believed the Lord heals but doesn't always choose to do so. He often said something like, "If you are a child of God, you'll either be healed in this life or the next." During one of his Bible classes, Walter Martin answered a question about healing and went on to share a personal story about my brother, Danny, who had once been ill with rheumatic fever:

> Well, God ordains the means and the ends. The means towards the salvation of mankind (that's the end) is the preaching of the gospel, and the means to the healing of the sick is by prayer and by meeting God's requirements in the Scripture. Now we have healings in our Bible class here all the time. We don't go out and blow trumpets outside and tell everybody about it, because if we started to, we'd be having the class out on the lawn — because there'd be that many people. We're not trying to attract attention to it, but there are people sitting here this morning that have been miraculously healed in this Bible class; put up your hands. You've come down; you've been anointed with oil. Now, we just have a great turnover in the class regularly. There are people right here; I've got people who were healed instantly of nicotine addiction. They smoked for thirty years, came into the class one morning, and said, "I can't take it anymore." I anointed them with oil, in the Lord, and they haven't smoked a cigarette again. We have alcoholics who have the same problem, and drug addicts. We had a drug addict who worked for the Christian Research Institute [CRI] and had a remarkable conversion experience. God just took the heroin away — instantaneously. No cold turkey, no shaking, no perspiration, no screaming, no cramps, no howls, no flying beetles, and crawling snakes, or anything at all. Just, Jesus Christ gave peace! It was gone. The addiction just disappeared. We have this happening all the time in divine healing, and so we have to encourage this. We have to believe in this — in the Lord's work — and we have to encourage people, where prayer is concerned.
>
> If you want healing, you should ask God for healing, and let God make the choice. Then, do everything that you're supposed to do to be sure that you haven't left anything undone. If God says, "Call for the elders and be anointed with oil in the name of the Lord," don't improve upon Him and say, "Well, that really isn't necessary in our day; we'll just have prayer." No! You'll never know what God *would have done* if you do not do *everything* God said to do. That's something always to remember. You'll never know, but if you do everything God said to do and have the faith to trust Him for it, the decision is His. If the person dies, you know that you have done everything

possible — *and it was their time* — but many times God intervenes in a remarkable way and heals.

My son Daniel was miraculously healed of rheumatic fever. He was diagnosed, being treated for it, and we prayed for him, *and God didn't heal him.* A friend of mine was in town, and I knew he exercised the gift of healing on occasion, remarkably, and I said, "Would you come over and see if the gift of healing will operate for my son?"

He said, "You can pray for him. The Lord uses you, too."

I said, "Yeah, but maybe I'm too close to the forest to see the trees. *Maybe this is something you have to do* — God has to use *you* to do." He came over, and he laid hands on Daniel.

Danny was healed in thirty seconds! The fever broke. He perspired through his pajamas. He was shaking all over. He looked up after we finished praying — after Bob finished praying — for him and said, "Gee, I'd like to go outside and play now." Here's a kid that couldn't move his joints, that was taking penicillin, and was, thirty seconds before, a diagnosed rheumatic fever case. The rest of his life he would have had to live on penicillin. We took him back [to the doctor] and ran him through all of the tests.

The doctor took off his glasses and cried. He says, "I'm a Roman Catholic. I don't go to church, but I support Billy Graham."

I said, "Well, that's good. Glad you do that."

He says, "'But I want you to know I'm going back to church again, now, because I've heard about this in my healing work as a doctor, for years. I've heard people come and tell me this, Christians particularly, and I just didn't believe it. God rubbed my nose in it this morning." He's crying. "I just got to thank God for that — it's a miracle!"

[I remember the day the Lord healed my brother, Danny. It was something I would never forget. We knew, without a doubt, that God had moved there.]

So, I've seen things happen. I prayed for some people, and they got sicker. I prayed for others; they died. And I prayed for others, and they were miraculously healed. So, God says, "Do it!" You get a bonus along the way when He talks to you and says, "I'm going to heal this one," and you know it in advance; that's even better! He's done that for me sometimes, but most of the time, it's "Do what I tell you to do, and then let me make the decision." And then that saves a lot of recriminations.

As a friend of mine used to say, "Don't be embarrassed to pray for the sick. It's God's kingdom. *He* should worry." In other words, don't be embarrassed about what's happening. If my embarrassment is going to engender, it's going to God, because He's the one who has to make the decision. You just do what you're supposed to do, and don't feel embarrassed about it.

So, I would say pray for that person's healing. Most of all, if they're not a Christian, pray for their salvation, but if they are a Christian, pray for their healing that they may be used of God. *There are people God wants sick.*

You say, "How do you know that?" I know because the Scripture teaches that, *and there are some people God wants dead.* And all the prayers in the world, all the faith claiming, teaching, positive confession, and positive thinking isn't going to save them, *because that's their time.* There is a time to be born, says Solomon, and there is a time to...what? — die!

You say, "Does God *really* want some people sick?" Yes, He wants them sick to learn a lesson. Sometimes people don't learn anything except by getting sick, and I'm one of them. I was pushing myself to death a few years ago, and the Lord slapped me down in a hospital bed. The doctors came in and stood around my bed — six of them — with long faces. I thought, "Well, this is it! I've had it." I didn't feel badly about it at all. After all, absent from the body, at home with the Lord. That wouldn't bother me any. I was just worried about *how* it was going to happen.

Here was this big amazing clinic — with six doctors standing there reading off these reports — and one of them said, "Dr. Martin, for a man who has so consistently abused his body for so long, you're in remarkably good shape."

[*Walter Martin laughs heartily*] "Praise the Lord for that! And, this slowed me down; I wouldn't have learned had I not been there. And I praise God for that. So, you have to learn lessons — sometimes the hard way.[1]

Although Walter Martin had to travel a lot for ministry reasons, he carved out time for his family as much as possible. My parents had been careful to pick out a home in an area worthy of a Norman Rockwell painting — an idyllic setting for many beautiful memories. On the wall of our living room hung a painted portrait of me, at the age of two. A narrow bubbling brook

---

[1] Recording of Walter Martin's Bible class. Cindee Martin Morgan, "Dr. Martin Mentions Son Danny, While Answering a Question about Healing," YouTube audio clip, 6:47, published December 29, 2008, https://www.youtube.com/watch?v=01Fopy-eb_E&t=81s.

ran through our front yard. As a child, my parents often found me perched on a rock next to its small tunnel, capturing frogs that must have lived in fear of me. Behind our house was an enormous hill that led to our dense woods. I remember sledding in the winter, and in the summer playing beneath towering trees I loved to climb.

On Eagle Crest Place, more than fifty years ago, my dad taught me to ride my first bike. At last able to afford new bikes for us, our parents took us to the local hardware store and allowed us to pick out our favorites. The excitement I felt that day was off the charts. I remember the smell of a new bike, the feeling of getting on it for the first time and hanging onto my father for dear life. He didn't think I needed training wheels; he was right. Before long, I had the hang of it. I can still see my dad watching me as I showed off my newest accomplishment.

Summer memories of Steal the Flag, catching lightning bugs, hanging out with treasured friends in our neighborhood, biking, forts built into trees, jump rope (with a rope so long eight children could jump in), and our family outings at a nearby lake will not soon be forgotten. Our parents had a swimming pool installed that became very popular in our neighborhood. At the end of our unusually long-necked cul-de-sac stood a basketball hoop my father had installed for all the children living on our street (which were many). From time to time, my dad played baseball and basketball with my brothers, along with the other neighborhood children. The basketball court became a sentimental landmark and, minus the hoop, remains there to this day.

Back in the 1960s, like most kids, we were told to be in when the streetlights went on. Not having complete success with this method, our parents bought a 10-inch-tall bell and rang it when the sun was setting. Some of our neighbors liked the idea so much they bought their own to summon their children. We all knew whose bell was whose. I am blessed to have custody of the Martin bell. It is a sweet reminder of the days the world seemed safer, doors often remained unlocked, and neighbors were in and out of each other's houses on a regular basis.

Strangely enough, I was unafraid as I once watched my dad shoot a large muskrat that had dared to set up house on the Martin homestead. I don't think PETA was around yet to protest. One year we had bats in our attic (common to the area). Breathing deep sighs of relief, our family watched them make a mass exodus from a tiny opening near the roof after being promptly evicted.

Our family golden retriever, Sandy, was often by my side and waited for me at my school bus stop in the afternoons. She was equally attentive to the rest of the Martin family and even managed to win the hearts of our entire neighborhood. Our German shepherd, Prince, would not have this legacy. Prince was loving and loyal — exclusively to the Martin family. Anyone else took care to stay away from his doghouse and well-protected play area when he was outdoors. He was the watchdog our golden retriever never was; Sandy would have happily showed intruders where the silver was kept if they stopped to pet or feed her. Both of my parents were cat lovers, so we had our share of them through the years. They roamed freely in and out of the house; they were part of the family yet enjoyed their autonomy.

My father always took time to watch a TV show or two with our family during evenings home from his travels. My siblings and I fought over whose turn it was to sit in the big recliner chair, next to Daddy. Two of our family's favorite shows were *Star Trek* and *The Munsters*. Walter Martin and his offspring were huge William Shatner fans. Once in a while, our dad even allowed us to watch a *Perry Mason* episode with him. The courtroom, after all, was in his blood.

Every time we left our house, our dad would pray and ask the Lord for a safe journey. My parents were always acknowledging God in our lives. In 1965, our family had grown to seven. My parent's new baby on board was a daughter they named Elaine, after our mom. Nearly every summer we went on vacation. We visited Canada and California, and we were elated when we first experienced Disneyland. I recall riding the Skyway with my dad and a couple siblings. As we glided across the park, my father briefly stood up and cheerfully insisted, "There isn't anything to be afraid of, kids!" He quickly sat down, upon seeing the look on my face. The effort to ease my fear of heights wasn't successful, but he did make me laugh at his failed attempt at humor and created a fun memory of a historic ride that allowed you to view the park from the air.

One of our most unusual vacations was our road trip to Florida. For Walter Martin, this was actually an extended speaking engagement that my parents turned into a family vacation. My father had been asked to be a substitute preacher at a Presbyterian church in Key Biscayne. We rented a house there for an entire month; I remember the day we headed to Florida and the hilarious scene I witnessed. Our luggage was neatly packed on the roof of our station wagon — temporarily — until we got on the freeway. The wind seemed out to get us that day. It was not long before we saw clothes and suitcases bouncing down the street like rubber balls. My parents groaned when they realized they were *ours*! My father quickly pulled over to rescue our luggage. I can still see my parents frantically trying to retrieve our clothing and suitcases. My parents took it in stride, having a great sense of humor; I don't believe you can survive raising five children without one.

A couple highlights of our Florida vacation were being able to visit our Uncle George and his family in Key Biscayne and going to Busch Gardens in Tampa Bay, where I recall thinking that I'd never seen so many pretty flowers, and, "What else is there to do here?"

Another fond memory of our time in Florida was when we were eating at a diner and had the opportunity to meet the two child stars of the television series *Flipper,* whose character names were Sandy (Luke Halpin) and Bud (Tommy Norden). I remember them politely shaking hands with my dad and smiling at us. This brought our vacation, for the Martin children, to a whole new level, as we were caught up in the novelty of meeting people from a television show we liked. I doubt those actors ever knew they had met the *Bible Answer Man.*

Walter Martin was also a wonderful uncle. My cousin June shared with me — when my father was teaching her to play golf — how she accidentally hit him right in the nose with the club! She almost broke it. When he returned from the doctor, he tracked down his niece and reassured her it wasn't her fault; he took the blame. June was blessed by his kindness and concern for her.

CRI's first official headquarters was in Wayne, New Jersey, about seven or eight miles from our home. Our father drove my siblings and me there from time to time so we could see where Daddy worked and hear more about what the Lord was doing through this ministry. I recall seeing our Uncle Tony and Walter Bjorck Jr. busy at work. Rows of bookcases, filled with books and research material, towered over us. As a child, I was pleased when I noticed the toads outside the building. I managed to catch one and accidentally dropped it down the window opening of our station wagon during one of the times my siblings and I waited for our father. (Thankfully, to the best of my knowledge, my father never knew.) The weight of what he did at CRI was somewhat lost on his five-year-old daughter.

I would one day learn, and better appreciate, that the purpose of CRI was to equip Christians to better defend their faith, to alert the body of Christ as to what a cult is, and how to witness to people led astray by them. Walter Martin's research staff began to steadily increase which helped widen CRI's scope of ministry. My grandmother, Martha Murphy, became CRI's first bookkeeper in between times she was sharing the gospel and singing at a gospel mission in Paterson, New Jersey. She was a humble soul, who my mother once mentioned was the first Christian woman to sing on Christian radio. She was so proud of her mom. My grandmother sang every Tuesday morning on WAAM. When my brother, Danny, and I were young, Gram took us to an American Rescue Workers meeting where we sang the hymn "What a Friend We Have in Jesus" to the poor and homeless people gathered there. I can remember barely being able to see over the podium. My grandmother was also a constant support to my parents on the home front. She often led me in prayers that always included "God bless CRI and all its efforts." She loved this ministry.

As in every family, storm clouds form, bringing with them challenging trials. One of the biggest ones we faced was when we almost lost my sister Elaine, who was only two and a half at the time. My mother had planned a lovely family reunion. Relatives came from everywhere. All were caught up in the excitement the day promised. I recall running around our house with much-loved cousins we rarely saw. Three had parents who worked for Trans World Radio, and were abroad some, so it was a treat when we got to see them. The adults were enjoying the fellowship, too.

It was a beautiful day; smells of delicious food filled the air. Shortly after the dinner hour, I recall seeing a few of my siblings and cousins hiding under a long buffet table that stood against our dining room wall. Unnoticed by almost everyone, the youngest member of our family — clad only in a diaper — tried to sneak under the far end of the table, to join those hidden there, having been denied access by the older children due to how crowded it was. To our horror, my baby sister crawled directly under where a tall copper coffee pot sat. I will never forget the sound of her screaming in agony as the pot tipped over and hot coffee rained down on her. Our brother Bryan (twelve at the time) immediately grabbed Elaine in that moment and — by the mercy of God—pulled her away from the scalding coffee just in time to keep her head and upper body from being burned as well. Doctors later told my parents that this saved Elaine's life.

Two of my uncles, seated close by, rushed her to a bathroom where my mother hurried to fill the tub with cool water. Tears ran down my mom's cheeks as she tried to comfort her child who had sustained life-threatening burns. My baby sister shook uncontrollably as she cried, "I sorry, Mommy!" believing she had done something wrong. Someone ran to a neighbor for more ice to put in the tub.

My parents were devastated as my father frantically made plans to get their toddler to the hospital. For several days they wondered if their youngest child would pull through; she had suffered third-degree burns over much of her tiny body. I recall my parents practically living at the hospital and my mother asking me to gather toys to entertain my sister. My father would drive the rest of my siblings and me there. My mom would hold Elaine up to the window — from her room a few floors up — as we waved from the parking lot and blew them kisses. Hospital rules were strict in those days; we were not allowed up to her room. Even so, the Lord comforted our family in an unusual way. My parents shared with us how Elaine's night nurses told them they could hear my sister softly singing in the middle of the night, "Jesus loves me, this I know, for the Bible tells me so. Little ones to Him belong. They are weak, but He is strong." To this day, this memory brings tears to my eyes. Even in intense pain, my baby sister was singing the words of truth our parents had taught us and, without even being aware of it, was being used by God to be a witness for Christ to all who could hear her.

After a lengthy stay in the hospital, and countless prayers, my parents were able to bring their baby home. I remember feeling tremendous joy as I watched her giggling, wrapped in white gauze bandages and bouncing in her crib as she held on to the side of it for dear life. This little girl was elated to be home at last. I couldn't stop kissing my baby sister; this reunion was better than any Christmas gift I'd ever been given. The Lord was merciful to our family and had brought us safely back together again.

In the Martin household, Saturday was renamed "Daddy's day." It really should have been called "Mommy's day," as it was the day our father often gave my mother a break from their five young children. I think part of their thinking, also, was to help us to make special memories with our dad, since he traveled often for ministry reasons.

After chores, we would usually go out for lunch. Our small town's Chuck Hut, Dairy Queen Brazier, and a nearby IHOP were our favorites. Danny and I, before leaving the restaurants, occasionally ate little packets of white sugar or used them to make concoctions we'd created at our table which included ketchup, salt, pepper, and whatever else we could lay hands on when we'd finished our meals. This was usually met with a stern look from our father and a promise of consequences should we not turn from our ways. When it was time to pay the bill, one of our favorite things to do was to guess the check. Bryan always announced the winner; whoever came the closest received the grand prize — a pack of gum.

One of my most unusual memories was when our family once left an IHOP. If our dad had no ability to laugh at himself, I would not share this story. The opposite was true; he was quick to point out the funny side of life and didn't hesitate to use self-deprecating humor. I loved this about him, and it taught me to not take myself so seriously. As we left the IHOP, a strong wind hit us full in the face. All of a sudden, our father shouted, "Quick, kids! Get Daddy's hair!" We chased a toupee that seemed to have a mind of its own as it sailed across the parking lot. To my dad's relief, we quickly recovered it. I suspect, at that moment, he was especially thankful to have *five* children.

After lunch, we could choose between several activities such as bowling, swimming, shopping, the zoo, the park, or a movie. At times, our dad would take us shopping at the Five and Ten store in town if we needed something. It seemed to have a little bit of everything. A fishbowl filled with one-cent Bazooka bubble gum sat eye level with most of our faces. We usually were each allowed a handful. My brothers also loved getting baseball cards there and the gum that came with them. Occasionally our father would take us to Buster Brown Shoes and buy us a pair of Keds sneakers. (Keds commercials had convinced the Martin children we could run faster in them.) We had so much fun with our father I recall not wanting to have many sleepovers with friends; I didn't want to miss the time with our family. I especially enjoyed when we'd go bowling. Getting our bowling shoes and finding the best ball seemed a highlight when your age is still in the single digits. It never occurred to me to complain about having to wear shoes so many feet had worn before me. Whenever we bowled, we usually were allowed to buy drinks and snacks. My father usually enjoyed bowling with us. He'd aim at the pins — while, at times, his kids fought about God knows what when his back was turned. The trick was *not* to get caught. Danny and I, especially, were full of it. If caught, we lived to regret it — that we got caught.

Even the time spent in the car was entertaining. My father would teach us old songs, like "Daisy, Daisy, Give Me Your Answer True," and "I've Been Working on the Railroad." He would make up silly lyrics to popular tunes, inserting the names of each of his children (something I later did with mine) and devoted a whole song to each of us. Mine was "Oh, Cindee Lynn, my Cindee Lynn...." This was truly a gift he gave us. We learned to laugh at ourselves, and each other, in a way that was healthy and entertaining. I've come to see that part of what keeps you sane is being able to find the humor in life, knowing the Lord *is* in control and *is* working *all* things for our good and for His glory.

During the long winter months, there were two words that lit up the lives of the Martin children — "snow day". If it was snowing at the break of dawn on a school day, my brother Bryan would turn on WABC radio to tune in to the latest weather report that would determine our fate. A snow day meant sleigh riding down the enormous hill that loomed over our backyard. It meant building igloos, making snow angels, snowmen, snowball fights, and eating icicles. It was a time like no other — a winter wonderland every child appreciates.

Early on, my father made his children aware of spiritual warfare. As soldiers of the cross know, sad days do come as a direct result of sharing the gospel. Those who oppose the message of the cross will oppose you; you will be attacked. It's not a matter of *if* but *when*. One afternoon, a newspaper reporter came to our door when my oldest brother, Bryan, was babysitting. He told us he was writing a nice story about our dad, and could we please answer some questions. Bryan told him our parents were not home, but the reporter pressed, and we gave in. We were excited to hear that our dad would be in the newspaper; we were proud that a reporter was writing about him. But when the story came out, it was anything but true or flattering. It was painful to learn our neighbors were reading it, too. It was, in a real sense, our family's first introduction to "fake news" and the bias that liberals in the press have toward Christians. *The National Enquirer* wasn't especially kind to my father, either. Serving the Lord comes with a price. My father weathered many storms — then and in the years to come. When you are a child of God, your armor gets damaged, and wounds can cut deep. He taught us it's all a part of running the race God has set before us.

The day my parents took us house hunting is a bittersweet memory. They were considering buying a charming Tudor that was, at the time, the most beautiful home I'd ever seen. I was nine years old and remember asking if one of the rooms could be mine. My parents seemed to love the house, too. Within weeks of the excitement of that happy day, I witnessed the end of an era for the Martin family as we once knew it. My parents separated for a season and later divorced. Out of love, respect, and a desire to honor them — now both home with the Lord — I will not discuss the reason this occurred. One thing it helped to teach me is that all those who are saved by grace battle with sin on a daily basis. I learned that, as Christians, the goal is to sin less as we grow in grace, but sanctification takes time. When we fail, God is faithful to complete the work He began in us. In spite of the "perfect storm" that hit our family head-on, I know that we had parents who loved the Lord and their children. Both my parents remarried Christians. Out of those unions, we were blessed with another sister, Debbie, from my father's new marriage, and three stepsisters from my mother's. The Lord *is* merciful to heal what is broken and to mend hearts whose trust is in Him. It wasn't always smooth sailing for any of us — and isn't to this day — but my hope is in the Lord.

3

NEW BEGINNINGS:
CRI ON THE WORLD STAGE

On the ministry front, my father continued to speak in churches. The Lord gave CRI wings to soar to greater heights. Before long, he appeared on both secular and religious television programs. In 1974, he moved CRI to the West Coast (California), a place he had always wanted to live. He'd grown tired of cold temperatures and shoveling snow. When our family first moved to San Juan Capistrano, a place my father jokingly referred to as paradise, he took us to the San Juan Mission and told us how the swallows migrated to our town every year, traveling six thousand miles from Argentina. He always brought to life the world around us.

Walter Martin became professor of Comparative Religion and Apologetics at Melodyland School of Theology in Anaheim, teaching on the cults and the occult. He also taught at the Simon Greenleaf School of Law, in Costa Mesa.[1]

The following year, he began broadcasting the *Bible Answer Man* program from Southern California. As a young teen, I met Elliot Miller, CRI's future editor-in-chief of its award-winning *Christian Research Journal*. I also met then-newlywed Bob and Gretchen Passantino. Walter Martin immediately saw their ministry potential once mentioning to me that Gretchen had "a brilliant mind."

One of my earliest memories of our new life on the West Coast is when my dad drove us to Tijuana, Mexico, for the first time. I still have the

---

[1] "A Brief Chronology of Walter R. Martin's Ministry," *Christian Research Newsletter* 2, no. 4 (1989), 4.

turquoise ring he purchased for me there. He firmly told us not to drink the water and to bargain over prices if we wanted to buy something. My father loved to bargain. He found a large 3-D wall hanging that a merchant convinced him was one-of-a-kind. He later laughed when he told me he'd learned that his one-of-a-kind steal of a deal was mass-produced in Mexico. Nonetheless, he was happy to have it!

Another fond memory I have of my Dad is when he flew our family to Hawaii one summer. In my mind's eye, I can still see him wearing his Hawaiian shirt with colors so bright they almost glowed in the dark. They alerted all who saw him he was a tourist. (It didn't concern him in the least there were Hawaiians holding up signs that read, "tourist go home.") Being a typical teen, I was entertained by his attire, only to decades later have this memory evolve into one of the sweetest ones I have of my father. He was indeed comfortable in his own skin.

My father and stepmother Darlene bought their second home in San Juan Capistrano when Darlene was expecting my sister Debbie. When I first held my new sister, it helped heal some of the heartache I felt — sadness most children have to process when their parents get divorced. I immediately fell in love with the youngest member of the Martin family. Debbie's middle name was "Joy," and she lived up to it. (Fifteen years later, I gave my youngest child, Katie, the same middle name, in honor of her aunt.) When Debbie was a toddler, I wrote a song for her that described our time together. My father once looked at Debbie and said to me, "You were just as cute, and I loved you — love you — just as much." That resonated with me; he needed me to understand that no matter what trials we faced his love was here to stay. As a teen, it was interesting to see my dad interact with Debbie, because it gave me a deeper appreciation of the kind of father he was. He always reminded me of his love — that, in spite of a divorce that grieved both my parents, we would always be a family. He was a peacemaker; his life demonstrated this. His heart's door was always open to biblical reconciliation and healing with others, both within and outside of the body of Christ. His obedience to the Lord in this way has had enormous impact on my life. I learned that we should not let the sun go down on our anger and give the devil a stronghold.[2]

On the other side of my life, with my mother, I grew particularly close to my stepsister Helene, whose sisterly love, devotion, and forgiving heart caused me to believe there wasn't any "step" in the word "stepsister"; I treasure her to this day. The Lord was busy working everything for the good of our now blended families — for both of my parents, their new spouses, and all of the children. God's loving providence in our lives reminds me of the words to the beautiful hymn by William Cowper, "God Moves in a

---

[2] See Ephesians 4:26–27.

Mysterious Way":

> God moves in a mysterious way His wonders to perform; He plants his footsteps in the sea and rides upon the storm.
>
> Deep in unfathomable mines of never-failing skill; He treasures up his bright designs, and works His sov'reign will.
>
> Ye fearful saints, fresh courage take; the clouds ye so much dread are big with mercy and shall break in blessings on your head.
>
> Judge not the Lord by feeble sense, but trust Him for His grace; behind a frowning providence He hides a smiling face.
>
> His purposes will ripen fast, unfolding every hour; the bud may have a bitter taste, but sweet will be the flow'r.
>
> Blind unbelief is sure to err, and scan His work in vain; God is His own interpreter, and He will make it plain.[3]

My father mentioned that our home in San Juan Capistrano previously had been owned and/or built by a Mormon. Although he taught that Mormonism is a cult, Walter Martin loved the people and didn't shrink back from associating or doing business with them. He liked to shop at Albertsons — a Mormon-owned grocery store — close to our home. This was a good example to everyone who knew him that we should love the cultist and be ready to give an answer for the hope we have, with gentleness and respect.[4]

It was exciting to see the secular world look to Walter Martin and CRI for answers. One time that stands out is in the wake of the 1978 Jonestown massacre. NBC interviewed my father, as the world grappled to make sense of how the cult leader, Jim Jones, could lead more than nine hundred people to their deaths.

Here is an excerpt from my father's exchange with an NBC reporter:

RITA: An American congressman murdered. Three American journalists murdered. More than four hundred men, women, and children committed suicide or are murdered; a tragedy unparalleled in history....It was a place of public beatings, public humiliations....Why did they stay? Why did they

---

[3] William Cowper, "God Moves in a Mysterious Way," Hymnary, 1774, https://hymnary.org/hymn/HTLG2017/325.
[4] See 1 Peter 3:15.

submit to a Jim Jones? Why did so many die at Jonestown?

WALTER: The person is conditioned into this gradually — isolated, indoctrinated, made dependent, and then taught that everybody who contradicts this is indeed their enemy. They develop what could be called a religious paranoia in which everybody's against us, so we all hang together.

RITA: How are they made, though, to believe this to the point where they give up life savings, they give up property, and then go do something that's touted as the Promised Land, and end up committing suicide or murder?

WALTER: They reach out for whatever's going to meet that need at the moment. They place their faith in that person; mistaken, zealous, dedicated faith. The person leads them away from any previous authority figure, and suddenly they are trapped by the fact that they have no place else to go; they can't go back. And, down there in Guyana, what you had was the ultimate logical conclusion. The homicidal and the suicidal tendency when a person inevitably gets so pushed and so isolated and puts so much confidence in another human being that they become dependent upon them to the point of life and death.

RITA: These, of course, are only possible partial answers, possible partial explanations. The world, after all, has never fully understood how an Adolph Hitler happened. Though we are left with a lack of comprehension, perhaps Jonestown did briefly shake us out of complacency.[5]

The brief interview can be seen on our ministry YouTube channel Walter Martin Jude 3. Watching it again, I am reminded of the nightmare this cult inflicted on people no doubt trying to find meaning and purpose in their lives, only to be manipulated, robbed, humiliated, and have their lives stolen from them.

When I heard about one of the stars from the series *Smallville* involved in a cult called Nxivm,[6] I immediately was reminded of Jonestown. While the cult this actress was involved in was much smaller and didn't murder their members, some of the control tactics sounded familiar. While I don't excuse her dark actions, my heart goes out to anyone trapped inside a cult. People

---

[5] Interview with Walter Martin by NBC Reporter Rita Diamond. WalterMartinJude3, "NBC – Jim Jones 'Atrocities' – Dr. Walter Martin Interview," YouTube video, May 23, 2011, https://www.youtube.com/watch?v=-CR_znjEurU.

[6] Kevin Fitzpatrick, "*Smallville* Star Turns to Scientology Precedent in NXIVM Cult Case," Vanity Fair, December 30, 2018, https://www.vanityfair.com/style/2018/12/allison-mack-nxivm-scientology-court-case.

not deceived by them often can't understand how victims can assist in their own capture, and then cooperate while being used for evil. The truth is that life apart from Jesus Christ is vulnerable to all types of mind control and evil influences. "The heart is deceitful above all things, And desperately wicked. Who can know it?" (Jeremiah 17:9). People who don't know God have a void in their life they must fill with something, or someone. The sad truth, however, is that anything that takes the place of a relationship with our Creator is harmful and will never meet the need of the human soul; it cannot remedy our fallen condition. *We are lost and must be found in Jesus Christ, or we will spend an eternity in hell.* I am thankful my father helped to expose the cults, helped the church to combat them, and taught the body of Christ how to share the good news of the gospel with cultists.

I was reminded, yet again, how the Lord continues to use Walter Martin to speak to a new generation about the cults when my youngest daughter, Katie, tuned in to Season 1 of *Wild Wild Country* on Netflix, documenting the Hindu-based Rajneesh cult. Katie was pleasantly surprised to see her grandad's face briefly pop up and to hear him commenting on this cult decades earlier: "Rajneesh is, biblically speaking, an anti-Christ that the Christian church should be aware of and prepared to answer with the truth."[7] To this day, the good works the Lord did through Walter Martin live on *as he dwells in his Father's house!* This is a powerful reminder that when we leave this world, works done in Jesus name may continue to touch others in this life if we, too, are faithful servants of our King.

Walter Martin was gaining national respect and eventually was dubbed "the father of the cult and countercult movement." CRI continued to blossom. Walter Martin founded FORWARD magazine, which was later renamed *Christian Research Journal.*[8]

Being in ministry full time, my dad was no stranger to odd forms of spiritual warfare. He had even received death threats. An experience at our home, while I was in my late teens, was particularly unsettling. We had an alarm system, so I never worried about intruders. This particular night, however, I woke up to cabinets — in the lower level of the house — opening and slamming shut, doors banging, and the sound of people walking around in the entryway and kitchen. *Our entire family was in bed. Asleep.* Knowing this, I froze with fear and initially could not move. I finally built up the courage to dart from my room to my father's, across the hall, and promptly woke him up. Seeing my look of terror and hearing the chaos going on downstairs, he

---

[7] *Wild Wild Country*, directed by Maclain Way and Chapman Way, Netflix, https://www.netflix.com/title/80145240.

[8] "A Brief Chronology of Walter R. Martin's Ministry," *Christian Research Newsletter* 2, no. 4 (1989), 4.

calmly raised his hand as he sought the Lord in prayer. In an authoritative voice, he said something like, "In the name of Jesus Christ, our Lord, leave this house...." Instantly, everything was quiet. I was comforted by how confident and unafraid my dad was. When we went downstairs, we found that *nothing was disturbed; all doors were locked*. I have never witnessed anything like this since. It was also a first for my father, but it didn't seem to faze him. I am thankful to have gone through this experience because it demonstrated to me — in an unforgettable way — that greater is He that is in me than he that is in the world (John 4:4). In telling this story, I recognize some people might now think of the Martin family as the Addams family — loveable but "they're creepy and they're kooky, mysterious and spooky." In all seriousness, I do think this supernatural experience is uplifting to share. It is yet another example of the power of God in the life of a believer, and it gives God glory. My father experienced many supernatural things while running the race, and his confidence in the Lord made me more confident.

One of my father's most famous public appearances was his 1980 interview on *The Phil Donahue Show*. Walter Martin debated Gavin and Yvonne Frost, founders of the Church of Wicca, and he powerfully defended the orthodox Christian position. The program opened with an incantation, followed by a large puff of smoke. Two clips of this historic exchange (that do not include the opening incantation) can be seen on our WalterMartinJude3 YouTube channel.[9] It was riveting. My father stood his ground and spoke the truth in love. I recall thinking, at the time, that Yvonne Frost looked like she needed an exorcism; it was chilling to see a couple so committed to the worship of Satan.

The most memorable moment was when Donahue said to my father, "I feel better about thinking about God saying to me, for example, 'Oh, come on in,' ya know? That's how I feel. Even, 'Look, you're not much, but come on in.' Isn't that a better sense of what God does?"

My father put his hand on Phil's shoulder and wisely replied, "Hey, I got something better than that. God said to Phil Donahue, almost two thousand years ago, in Jesus Christ, 'Come on in — you can come.'" Phil shot back, "Well, I know, but it just seems that it makes God an awfully stern taskmaster," to which Walter Martin responded, "No, it makes Him a just judge. Don't you want a just judge?"[10]

---

[9] WalterMartinJude3, "Dr. Walter Martin – *The Phil Donahue Show* Part 1/2," YouTube video, 7:33, published February 15, 2010, https://www.youtube.com/watch?v=3YA5la8Bnqk.

[10] WalterMartinJude3, "Dr. Walter Martin – *The Phil Donahue Show* Part 2/2," YouTube video, 9:44, published November 10, 2008, https://www.youtube.com/watch?v=SwsYTV1uqRU.

I remember watching this exchange between them, when it first aired, and being struck by how much God was using my father to be a bright light in the intense darkness. It also made me start praying for Phil Donahue.

4

WORKING FOR CRI, MEETING HAL LINDSEY, AND DISPENSATIONALISM

The year before I was married, I briefly worked for my father at CRI. Both of my brothers — Bryan and Danny — also shared this honor. Working for CRI gave me a window into the apologetic countercult world of Walter Martin. It gave me the opportunity to witness the theological wheels turning inside the ministry he founded and to be frequently reminded of my father's love for this ministry. It was riveting, and I was proud of my dad. I was a receptionist, but it gave me a front-row seat to much of what was happening there. Once in a while, while screening calls, I was asked if I knew Dr. Martin. That was always a fun question. From time to time I had the honor of transcribing letters by our researchers, written to those writing CRI with questions. One of my coworkers once commented to me that my father's mind was like a computer. Indeed, it was.

I will never forget the day Christian contemporary artist Keith Green called CRI, about a year prior to his untimely death. I was told that he was on the line speaking with one of the researchers. I was, and remain, a huge fan of Keith Green's powerful music. It deeply blessed me to know that he valued CRI and the *Bible Answer Man*. Someone later told me he'd mentioned Walter Martin to a crowd of college students, while ministering in music at Oral Roberts University. It is interesting how our lives and the lives of our loved ones crisscross with others in the body of Christ in ways we never imagined possible.

On many occasions, I would accompany my dad to his ever-expanding

Bible class when it was at Melodyland Christian Center, in Anaheim, California. During that season of our lives, he told me how loving the Charismatics are. While disagreeing with my father on peripheral issues, they embraced him at Melodyland, setting an impressive example for the body of Christ. My father loved his Bible class, and they loved their teacher. I can recall him standing behind the podium with a bucket (the size similar to a KFC one) filled with notes from his class. He would patiently read through several questions before preaching his sermon. Some of the notes were prayer requests. There were questions about doctrine, personal ones about his health, questions regarding other Christian leaders, questions about news stories, and sometimes comical comments my father would share out loud. Walter Martin knew how to capture the attention of everyone in the room. I enjoyed this side of my dad, who had an extremely charismatic personality.

My father once mentioned to our family that a television actor, Hayden Rorke, visited his Bible class from time to time. Rorke played Dr. Alfred Bellows on the popular *I Dream of Jeannie* show. This series was a favorite in the Martin household back in the sixties. Rorke gave my father a signed photo, of himself, for our family.

On one of the many occasions I attended my father's Bible class, I met future best-selling author (and Women of Faith speaker) Barbara Johnson. In later years, I was blessed to get to know her as a friend who encouraged me in my writing. Barbara Johnson became widely recognized in Christian literary circles as the "Christian Erma Bombeck." My father wrote the foreword to her compelling book *Where Does a Mother Go to Resign?* His words are profoundly uplifting and encouraging to the body of Christ, so I will share this excerpt. Walter Martin wrote:

> I first knew Barbara as the "lady with the sunshine smile" at our (Melodyland) Christian Center's hotline office. Later I learned of how God had, unknowingly to me, spoken to her through my Bible class to help her through the hard time when she first knew that her son was a homosexual. She has been one of the most faithful members of the Bible class....
>
> Read this book if you are hurting, if your family is hurting, or if you want to learn about triumph in tragedy, about the healing of a broken heart. At one time, Barbara wanted to resign from being a mother. Along with hundreds who have been helped by her, I am glad she didn't![1]

---

[1] Barbara Johnson, *Where Does a Mother Go to Resign?* (1978; repr., Bloomington, MN: Bethany House, 1994).

The Bible Answer Man
Walter Martin and Hank Hanegraaff

Dr. James Dobson later called Barbara Johnson's book, *Where Does a Mother Go to Resign?*, "one of the most incredible stories of courage under fire that I think I've ever heard."[2]

From time to time, I was blessed to hear Christian artists perform at Melodyland. One of my favorites was Andre Crouch, who was on fire for Christ. Hearing him sing the beautiful song "Through It All" blessed my life, as it did so many lives there. Another memory that also stands out was when I heard Katherine Kuhlman preach at Melodyland. Kuhlman was an American Pentecostal evangelist.[3] The experience was peculiar. She was dressed in a white gown, and her voice was loud and commanding. I was riveted to my chair; Katherine Kuhlman seemed to have light shining from her face as she glided about the stage. When she prayed for people during the service, *rows of them fell down* as she touched them. Some fell without her having to even lay hands on them. I didn't want to get anywhere near her, uncertain what to make of it. I had never seen anything like this in my life and haven't since. I was perplexed, at the time, if I was blessed to be there or was being warned about trusting everyone who claims to have the power of healing. While I do believe God can heal, in our day, *if He so chooses*, I remain a little skeptical regarding some who claim to have the gift. What was evident to me, however, was the love I witnessed that night for Jesus Christ and for one another. I decided I was content to leave my uncertainties with the Lord.

I remember the day my father introduced me to his friend Hal Lindsey, author of *The Late Great Planet Earth*, who was teaching at Melodyland during the same time he was. His relationship with Hal was memorable, to say the least. They publicly joked with one another about theology and had a mutual respect that made it possible to be friends, when they didn't always agree. My dad held to a post-tribulation view, which he taught is consistent with the beliefs held by the historical Christian church. In his sermon, "The Tribulation and the Church," he pleads for respect, civility, and forbearance for those who disagree in the area of eschatology. He also discussed his difference of opinion with Lindsey.

Having once had the threat of his microphone being cut at a church he spoke at — should he express his eschatological views — Walter Martin saw the need to encourage the body of Christ to treat one another with respect when these types of disagreements arise. Here is a small excerpt of one of his messages on the subject:

There have developed tremendous conflicts in the Body of Christ

---

[2] Johnson, *Where Does a Mother Go to Resign?*, front cover.
[3] "Kathryn Kuhlman," Wikipedia, https://en.wikipedia.org/wiki/Kathryn_Kuhlman.

> about the subject of the Second Coming of our Lord. And I think that what we ought to do is to have freedom to express ourselves without being penalized for our positions. And unfortunately, that's what's going on today....
>
> Now I don't know what frightens people so much about different points of view. The apostle Paul says that "there must needs be differences of opinions in your midst, so that the truth may be made known." There is nothing wrong with having different opinions. And ministers — not only myself but others — should not be penalized for taking what is, in the minds of some, an unpopular position.... Love, according to 1 Corinthians 13, is supposed to govern the activities and the function of the members of the body of Christ. And when I see Christians fighting among themselves, about whether Jesus is coming before the tribulation, the middle of the tribulation, or after the tribulation; when I see books being published where statements are made, "We are the generation that will see the Second Coming of Jesus Christ"; when I see this type of thing going on, and bitterness developing, a root of bitterness developing among Christians, then I think it's time for us to air our differences of opinions. I think it's time for us to give the other guy a break. If you don't agree with him, love him, or her, for Christ's sake. But don't make that a point of division in the Body of Christ.
>
> We must not be divided about whether we sprinkle, pour, or immerse, or whether we have wine, grape juice, or Coca Cola at the Communion service — which is what they do in Latin America anyhow. We shouldn't be arguing about pretribulation, midtribulation, and posttribulation, and premillennial, amillennial, and postmillennial. The principle task of the church is to evangelize the lost world, and they couldn't care less.[4]

Dr. Martin then goes on in this sermon to explain the basis of his beliefs regarding the pretribulation rapture. He also describes a conversation he had with his friend Hal regarding their differing views:

> John places the first resurrection at the end of the tribulation and just before the millennium — perfectly consistent with Paul, perfectly consistent with Christ, and perfect fulfillment of Daniel. I believe this is important for us to understand because we have been

---

[4] WalterMartinJude3, "Dr. Walter Martin: The Tribulation and the Church, Pt. 1 of 6," YouTube video, 10:00, published February 21, 2010, https://www.youtube.com/watch?v=SA_rEAX0aeE.

hearing only one view, primarily, for 140 years, and it is not the historic view of the Christian church. I find it to be completely in disagreement with Matthew 24. It surely is in disagreement with 2 Thessalonians 1 and 2. It will not stand up in Revelation chapter 20, and therefore, it should be rejected. Now, let me be careful here. If you want to be a pretribulationist or a midtribulationist, the Lord bless you. That's your decision, and I sure do hope you're right....I tell Lindsey every time we talk about this, "I sure hope to heaven you're right!"

And he said, "Well, if I'm wrong, I'm coming looking for you! By that time, you should have it pretty worked out what we're going to do."

I said, "Don't come looking for me, because as soon as I see the abomination that makes desolate, Walter is going to split!" That's what Jesus said, and that's common sense! Now, when Hal and I discuss things, I find that there are certain things common to pretribulationists after I present something like this. They say to me, inevitably, "But, Walter, *you do not understand.* Matthew chapter 24 and 2 Thessalonians chapter 2 are all talking about the tribulation saints — the church during the tribulation period. It's not talking about the church universal, as it is today. These are the tribulation saints." That's the argument. Here's the answer: God is never illogical. Make a note of that. God is never illogical. He is sometimes alogical — which means He goes beyond logic — but He is never illogical, because when you are illogical, you are not thinking straight. And God thinks straight. Now think about this for a moment. This is what I said to Hal:

"Hal, these are the tribulation saints?"

He said, "Right."

I said, "How do you know that they are the tribulation saints unless you have first assumed that the church is gone? And if you first assumed that the church is gone, you are illogical, because you are arguing in a circle. You are begging the question. It's illogical, and if it's illogical, *it is not the mind of God,*" to which I received no response. Nobody will give any response to it because the argument, itself, cannot be refuted. If you arbitrarily make these people the tribulation saints, the only way that you can do it is to assume that your position is right. And you can't assume that your position is right; you have to prove your position. Proof and assumption are two different things. Circular reasoning is very dangerous....Stop fighting and discriminating in the body of Christ.

The position I gave tonight is a very strong position. It's a very sound position in English, Greek, or Hebrew. It is sustained by all of the great minds of the church, for nineteen centuries, and it's not heretical. It's plain common sense…. You have got to go to the text itself and ask the question first, what did Jesus teach? What did Paul understand Jesus to teach? What did John understand Him to teach? What did the church fathers understand *them* to say? What did the Reformers and the Catholic theologians interpret it to mean? And after you get all of *that* evidence together, then you make a decision based upon the facts, and not upon emotion.

People who hold to the pretribulation position are pretty much psyched out by fear — that if anti-Christ comes, they're going to be persecuted — and they don't like it…. I once believed in the pretribulation rapture. So did Dr. Oswald Smith, one of Canada's greatest Bible teachers. After fifty years in the ministry — reading his Greek New Testament — Dr. Smith saw after the tribulation, and connected it with the apostle Paul, and reversed his position after fifty years, and wrote a beautiful pamphlet, *Tribulation or Rapture: Which?* They said he was senile. No, he was just willing to change a position he found would not stand up.[5]

Walter Martin's friendship with Hal Lindsey set a good example for the church of what it means to show one another grace, especially when it comes to what my father taught is peripheral doctrine. His unedited sermon "The Tribulation and the Church" can be heard on our WalterMartinJude3 YouTube channel.[6] It presents a historic view of eschatology held for centuries by the church, before dispensationalism was born.

It is important to note that Charles Spurgeon did not believe in dispensationalism; he thought the church would pass through the tribulation.

> While Spurgeon was clearly premillennial in his eschatology, he was most certainly not dispensational. The *sine qua non* of Dispensationalism, to which even the Progressive Dispensationalists agree, is the distinction between Israel and the Church. As [Timothy] Weber points out:

---

[5] WalterMartinJude3, "Dr. Walter Martin: The Tribulation and the Church," recorded sermon, YouTube audio clip, Parts 4 (9:54) and 5 (7:49), published February 21, 2010, https://www.youtube.com/watch?v=PaiTuOX2I1o and https://www.youtube.com/watch?v=5VHwLs6yhWM.

[6] WalterMartinJude3, "Dr. Walter Martin: The Tribulation and the Church," Part 1, YouTube video, 10:00, published February 21, 2010, https://www.youtube.com/watch?v=SA_rEAX0aeE.

What separated dispensationalists from their fellow futurists was their strict literalism when interpreting biblical prophecy, their absolute separation of Israel and the church as two distinct peoples of God, and some conclusions which grew out of these two presuppositions.

Spurgeon rejected any notion that separated the people of God into separate groups with separate purposes.[7]

During a question-and-answer time in his Bible class Dr. Martin discussed being on The Dennis Prager Show radio broadcast and afterward being accused of anti-Semitism:

> I'd like you to open your Bibles, if you will, to the book of Deuteronomy, chapter 30. [He then reads Deuteronomy 30:1–9 NKJV.]
>
> "Now it shall come to pass, when all these things come upon you, the blessing and the curse which I have set before you, and you call them to mind among all the nations where the LORD your God drives you, and you return to the LORD your God and obey His voice, according to all that I command you today, you and your children, with all your heart and with all your soul, that the LORD your God will bring you back from captivity, and have compassion on you, and gather you again from all the nations where the LORD your God has scattered you. If any of you are driven out to the farthest parts under heaven, from there the LORD your God will gather you, and from there He will bring you. Then the LORD your God will bring you to the land which your fathers possessed, and you shall possess it. He will prosper you and multiply you more than your fathers. And the LORD your God will circumcise your heart and the heart of your descendants, to love the LORD your God with all your heart and with all your soul that you may live.
>
> Also, the LORD your God will put all these curses on your enemies and on those who hate you, who persecuted you. And you will again obey the voice of the LORD and do all His commandments which I command you today. The LORD your God will make you abound in all the work of your hand, in the fruit of your body, in the increase of your livestock, and in the produce of

---

[7] Dennis M. Swanson, "Charles H. Spurgeon and the Nation of Israel: A Non-Dispensational Perspective on a Literal National Restoration," The Spurgeon Archive, http://archive.spurgeon.org/misc/eschat2.php.

your land for good. For the LORD will again rejoice over you for good as He rejoiced over your fathers, if you obey the voice of the LORD your God, to keep His commandments and His statutes which are written in this Book of the Law, and if you turn to the LORD your God with all your heart and with all your soul."

How many of you saw the *Los Angeles Times* Calendar write-up on the Christian Research Institute? I think he was very fair in the article by pointing out that I was accused of something I did not say — on the [Prager] program, I did not say that the Jews living *today* were responsible for the crucifixion of Jesus Christ. I said some Jews, living at the time of Jesus, conspired unjustly to put Him to death and with the Romans, they conspired and — finally — He was executed by the Romans. The Jews did not execute, but the Jews delivered Jesus Christ — an innocent victim — to be crucified. Then I quoted on the program the High Court of Israel's judgment on Adolph Eichmann.[8] They never proved that Eichmann personally ever killed a Jew. What they proved was that he knew about their deaths, consented to it, and did nothing to stop it.

So, the High Court of Israel ruled, "He that delivers an innocent person to die is more culpable or guilty than he that executes."

I said on the Prager program that the Romans did not have as great a guilt as the Jews and that it was the fault of the Jews, at that time, that Jesus was delivered. The Romans only acted as the executioners, and therefore the High Court of Israel decision condemned the Jews, at the time, because they delivered an innocent man to death. I said I was tired of everybody piling up on the Pontius Pilate balcony and washing their hands in his basin and saying, "I have nothing to do with the death of this just man." The fact of the matter is, that's history; that can't be changed.

I want to emphasize something; I think in light of all of Israel's publicity in the press and all of the problems that are going on there in the Middle East, the Christian ought to reconsider very carefully the Jew today is not suffering as a result of the crucifixion of Jesus Christ. That's not the primary cause of their suffering. Whether you're a Jew or you're a Gentile, if you consent to the fact that Jesus was a false Messiah and if you come against Him today — whether you're a Jew or a Gentile — you're a participant in that crucifixion though it took place two thousand years ago! That's fact. Jew and

---

[8] Adolf Eichmann was a Nazi SS Senior Assault Unit Leader and responsible for organizing the logistics involved with the Holocaust. See https://en.wikipedia.org/wiki/Adolf_Eichmann.

Gentile is guilty, equally before God if they turn away from the sacrifice of the cross. That's clear New Testament theology.

The real reason why the Jews have suffered, down through the ages, is often overlooked by Christians, and that's why I had our reading from the thirtieth chapter of Deuteronomy, where God says that He "will call the Jews back from all the nations where I have driven them." In other words, Israel was dispersed throughout the world in 70 AD. They were dispersed by the hands of the Roman empire, but under the direct command of God. You say, "How do you know that?" Because it says, "If any of thine be driven out of the outer most parts of heaven, from thence will the LORD thy God gather them and from there will He fetch them," but, in verse 3, it says, "The LORD thy God has scattered thee." So, it's imperative to understand that the hand of God is against Israel today in judgment because of what they did in disobedience to Him. The crucifixion of Jesus Christ was the capstone of their disobedience, but the entire structure of their disobedience is spelled out here in Deuteronomy chapter 30.

Do not ever make the mistake of believing that national Israel today, in Palestine or Israel, is the Israel of God, because they are not; they cannot be until they repent of their sin and until they confess that Jesus Christ is God and Savior — that He is truly the Messiah.

Now, it's very clear right here, "Thou shalt return unto the LORD thy God," verse 2, "and shall obey His voice according to all that I commanded thee this day, thou and thy children with all thine heart, and with all thine soul." That will take place. The time will come when they will return in fullness. There will be almost a national repentance. A large segment of the Jews will turn to Messiah and acknowledge Jesus Christ as the Son of God as their Savior. "And the LORD thy God will bring thee into the land which thy Fathers' possessed and thou shalt possess it and He will do thee good and multiply thee above thy Fathers." He has done that. He has brought them back into the land. He has multiplied them beyond anything they ever were before. He has crowned them with all kinds of material benefits. He's allowed them to progress to the place that they are and made them the most singularly powerful nation in the Middle East, right now — Israel. He did all the things He said he would do, but something has yet to be done, and that something is in verse 6. "The LORD thy God will circumcise thine heart." Now that's a very graphic picture. You don't need anybody to draw it out for you. God is going to do to their spiritual nature what the Jews do to their flesh: circumcision. He's going to cut off the excess skin of their souls, and He is going to crown them with the Abrahamic covenant. He's going to recognize them as His children, but that cannot take place until they have repented of their sins. You see, circumcision is equated with baptism in the New Testament as a seal of the covenant. Circumcision was the seal of the covenant in the Old Testament, and baptism, in the New Testament, became the seal that Christians recognize. It is an outward appearance, which testified to an inward conversion. That was the meaning of baptism. So, also with Israel; God will circumcise Israel, and He will do it spiritually. That's why the apostle Paul wrote, "One is not a Jew because he is a Jew outwardly, because of circumcision. Instead, he is a Jew inwardly who is a true Jew spiritually, and circumcision is of the heart" — the whole argument of Pauline theology — the Abraham covenant applicable to the Jew.

Today, the Christian church is receiving the blessings that Israel would have received because we have been grafted into the olive tree that Israel was broken off from. We are not to boast against Israel, not to look down on Israel because of their unbelief and their rebellion and not to treat them as if they have no part of the divine covenant. They do. They have a part of the covenant when God circumcises their hearts — when God restores them to a place of fellowship and of blessings. "The LORD thy God will circumcise thy hearts," verse 6, "and the hearts of thy children." So, it's talking about salvation to the Jew and to their children. "And, thou shalt love the LORD thy God with all thine heart, with all thine soul that you may live. And the LORD thy God will place the curses that He placed upon you, upon your enemies and on them that hate thee which persecuted thee."

Yasser Arafat, take notice. Take notice. God said, "I will deal with Israel. They are like the pupil of my eye — very sensitive — don't touch them. I will touch them; I will discipline them, not you." Therefore, it's very important to realize that the promise He made to Abraham He intends to keep. That promise was, "I will bless them that bless you. I will curse them that curse you." He still maintains that. Adolph Hitler was finished the day he launched his Jewish persecutions. It might have taken twelve years for him to die, but his Reich was all over with, as far as God was concerned. To touch the pupil of God's eye was to bring divine judgment. The Arabs are touching the pupil of God's eye today. They are going to receive divine judgment if they do not repent of it. And we are seeing today, on every side, this particular passage coming to pass. "Thou shalt return and obey the voice of the LORD and do all His commandments which I command you this day and the LORD thy God will make thee plenteous in every work of thine hand, in the fruit of thy body, in the fruit of thine cattle, in the fruit of thy land for good. The LORD will again rejoice over thee, for good, as He rejoiced over your Fathers — if you shall listen."

Now, notice this, it's a conditional promise, verse 10. People say, "God doesn't put strings on what He says." God has strings on things! For instance, God will not save you unless you repent. That's not a string; you're not going to get forgiven. God's love is unconditional. He loved us and redeemed us, but to continue in His love is conditional. He told you so in John, chapter 15. "You will continue in my love" if you what? What? [Hearing people in the class respond.] "Obey Me!" There's a big string right there. "You will continue being the beneficiary of my love" if you do what? "If you obey Me. If you don't, you're going to be the beneficiary of my justice. Even though I love you, you're still going to suffer."

"If thou shall harken to the voice of the LORD thy God to keep His commandments and His statutes which are written in the book of the law and if thou turn to the LORD thy God with all thine heart and with all thine soul. For this commandment, which I command thee this day it is not hidden from you" (says the Hebrew). Ah, God says, remember, I didn't place this up in heaven where you couldn't get at it. I gave it to you here on the Earth. I told you what I wanted you to do. It is not in heaven that thou should say "who shall go up to heaven and bring it down to us that we man hear and do it. These are beyond the sea that you should say who should go over the sea for us and bring it unto us that we may hear it and do it, but the Word is very near unto thee in thy mouth and in thy heart that you may do it."

Now, see, now listen, this is addressed directly to the Jew. "I have set before thee this day life and good and death and evil in that I command thee this day to love the LORD thy God, to walk in His ways, to keep His commandments and His statutes and His judgments that you may live. That you may multiply, and the LORD thy God shall bless thee in the land where thou goest to possess it." Now, I want you to look very closely at what God says He will do if Israel does not obey Him, and you will read through history right now.

"But if thine heart turn away so that thou wilt not hear but be drawn away and worship other gods and serve them, I denounce to you this day you shall surely perish. You shall not prolong your days in this land whether thou passes over Jordan to possess it." This is now a divine indictment, if you will: "I call heaven and earth to record this day against you. I have set before you life, death, blessing and cursing. Therefore, choose life that thou and thy seed may live. That thou mayest obey His voice. Cling to Him for He is thy life. Thy life and the length of thy days that thou mayest dwell in the land which the LORD swear unto the Fathers — to Abraham, to Isaac and unto Jacob to give them."

If you read back, chapter 28 and 29, you will find a whole series of curses, which God pronounced upon the Jews. "If thine would go after other gods, if thou would not obey His voice," if they would not do what He commanded them to do. So, let us be done forever with the error of thinking that the crucifixion of Jesus Christ was the reason for the Jewish suffering from the year of 70 AD to when they were dispersed 'til today. It is not. The reason that they are dispersed, the reason why they suffer, the reason why they will continue to be persecuted (and have to be drawn back into their own land) is because they have not obeyed the voice of Moses. That's why Jesus said to them, "You are always trying to point to Moses to judge Me. Well, remember something, it was Moses who wrote of Me." He summoned Moses against them, as a witness! This is not anti-Semitism. This is not anti-Jewish. This is good, solid biblical history, and the Christian doesn't have to hang his head and be ashamed of the fact that it's there. If it's anti-Semitic, Moses was the greatest anti-Semite of all time. If this is anti-Semitic, he's the greatest of them all because he comes against them — in the name of the LORD — and says, "I call heaven and earth to record today against you."

Now, I don't have the time to go into the fullest exposition I would like to. I would like to draw a parallel to this in our own lives. If the church is indeed the Israel of God, if as Romans 11 says, "we are the heirs of Abraham's covenant," and we have accepted the Messiah which the Jews rejected, then God speaks also to us. If He would not spare Israel, He surely will not spare the church. If we slide into apostasy, if we follow false doctrines, if we go and worship at the altar of other gods — or if we think we are gods — if we pervert His judgments and His Scriptures, then we will not escape any more than they escaped the judgment of God. That is why it says in the Scriptures, that judgment will begin at the house of the Lord. "And, if the righteous scarcely be saved, where shall the ungodly and the sinner make his appearance?" [1 Peter 4:18].

It is true, God loved the world and sent His Son to be our Savior.

It is true that Jesus Christ bore in His own body our sins on the tree. It is true that we have access into the holiest of all by the blood of Jesus. It is true that we are kept in the hollow of His hand. It is true that we are His sheep — but it is also true, according to Romans chapter 11, that if we fall into Israel's sin, that He will break us off from fellowship and break us off into judgment, just as well as the Jew. Boast not thyself against what happened to Israel. It can happen to you. [Referencing verse 18.] Remember, it can happen to you. Israel was not broken off from the covenant. Israel is taken out and will be grafted back in again when there is repentance. This is not anti-Semitism. This is good old solid biblical theology. I think that with all of the stuff that is going around today about the Jews and anti-Semitism (and all the things which Christians are walking around as if on eggshells), it's about time we dealt with the real issue. The real issue is the persecution of the Jew, down through the ages, has been the Jews' fault because the Jews rebelled against Moses's law and against the will of God. Because of that, the judgment of God came down!

...Let us pray for Israel. Let us pray that, surrounded by her enemies, that God will deliver her from the wrath which is to come. Let us pray for repentance toward God and faith in the Lord Jesus Christ. Let us stand with them against all the nations of the Earth to help them inherit the land which God has given them. But, let us not be so foolish as not to recognize the reasons for it and to be certain that we, who are standing by divine grace, should take heed, lest we fall. God has given us the model of the gospel. Let us share it with Israel and let us understand why this is necessary. "Except a man be born again, he cannot see the Kingdom of God" [John 3:3].[9]

Walter Martin respectfully unpacked church history for those who would take the time to consider it; he refuted dispensational views first introduced by John Darby in AD 1840 and later expanded on by others. He, himself, admits how he once believed it, only later to be convinced by what the church has taught for centuries. The Christian church was dividing on this subject long before my father's time, during his time, and continues to argue about dispensationalism to this day. This must grieve the heart of God. My father warned against dividing over eschatology because he recognized that the main focus of a believer in Jesus Christ is the Great Commission. Jesus said, "Therefore go and make disciples of all nations, baptizing them in the name

---

[9] From a recording of Walter Martin's Bible Study class, May 3, 1987. Copyright Christian Research Institute.

of the Father and of the Son and of the Holy Spirit, and teaching them to obey everything I have commanded you. And surely, I am with you always, to the very end of the age" (Matthew 28:19–20). Walter Martin held to the historical gospel passed down by our church father's centuries before dispensationalism was promoted from the pulpit, bookstores, and in the entertainment industry. Like Spurgeon before him, he exhorted the church to keep our eyes on Jesus and to prioritize 1 Peter 3:15: "But in your hearts honor Christ the Lord as holy, always being prepared to make a defense to anyone who asks you for a reason for the hope that is in you; yet do it with gentleness and respect." Whatever your eschatological position, Walter Martin's words are both timely and thought provoking.

For decades, I avoided eschatological arguments. I was troubled by the millions of dollars made on dramatic books and films that claim to have the best interpretation of the Bible, especially the Book of Revelation. This prompted me to become better acquainted with church history that addressed these issues. Did John Darby in the 1800s (who is considered the father of dispensationalism), along with others, unearth a treasure trove of truth that had been hidden for centuries from the church? Whatever the answer may be, it is spiritually unhealthy for Christians to be consumed with talk of the Rapture — especially when something bad happens — and seek to interpret what current headlines reveal, as if any of us possess an infallible theological crystal ball. The truth is, we don't; God didn't intend us to know the end from the beginning. Embracing the theory of a pretribulation rapture appears to provide an emotional ripcord, shifting the discussion to getting out of here rather than reaching the lost. While there is joy in encouraging one another that Jesus *is* coming again soon, to obsess or divide over eschatology minimizes and damages our focus on evangelism; I learned this from my father.

Some say that one of the litmus tests *to determine if you are saved* is if you believe in dispensationalism. Christians who are not dispensational are not allowed to teach in some of the churches that hold to that belief. I have heard Christians disparage other believers for not accepting views that, two-thousand years ago, were foreign to the church. These questions must be asked: has the church, in its modern days, developed a brand of eschatology (*added* to the gospel once delivered to the saints) that is causing division among us? Each of us must decide that in our own prayer closet. I am content to leave the future in God's hands. The Lord will take care of what is to come. "So do not worry about tomorrow; for tomorrow will care for itself. Each day has enough trouble of its own" (Matthew 6:34 NASB).

I have a healthy respect for the Book of Daniel and Revelation, and I believe in Christ's second coming. Without a doubt, biblical history, past, present, and future is encrypted in the Word of God and will come to pass as He has ordained. Those who set dates regarding Christ's return are disobeying what Scripture teaches and have led others astray. Jesus said, "But of that day and hour no one knows, not even the angels in heaven, nor the Son, but the Father alone" (Matthew 24:36 NASB). If we come into contact with date setters, we should not walk away from them; we should run — if there is not repentance.

I love those with whom I disagree. I have friends who are dispensational who also agree that we should not divide. We stand shoulder to shoulder as warriors of the cross. Our calling as Christians is to be a light to everyone in our path. "Let your light shine before others that they may see your good deeds and glorify your Father in heaven" (Matthew 5:16 NIV). Every opportunity the Lord provides is our personal mission field.

Charles Spurgeon said it well: "If sinners be damned, at least let them leap to Hell over our dead bodies. And if they perish, let them perish with our arms wrapped about their knees, imploring them to stay. If Hell must be filled, let it be filled in the teeth of our exertions, and let not one go unwarned and un-prayed for."[10] We must lead people to Christ while there is yet time. There is no calling greater on a Christian's life than to know Christ, and to make Him known.

---

[10] Charles Spurgeon, "The Wailing of Risca," sermon delivered on December 9, 1860, at Exeter Hall, Strand; available at https://www.spurgeongems.org/vols7-9/chs349.pdf.

The Bible Answer Man
Walter Martin and Hank Hanegraaff

My grandmother's home in Nutley, New Jersey, where my parents briefly lived in the attic. This is where my father conceived of the idea of CRI. 1952.

Rev. And Mrs. Walter Martin, Mr. and Mrs. Everett Jacobson, and Phyllis Jacobson. *Bride and Groom* Show. CBS, 1953. (David Pickoff, Photographer.)

My favorite photograph of my father and me. 1963.

My father and mother with me and my siblings: Bryan, Jill, Daniel, and Elaine. Oakland, New Jersey. 1966.

Rev. and Mrs. Walter Martin with their children at Van Riper Ellis Memorial church in Fairlawn, New Jersey. Circa 1968.

The Christian Research Institute, Wayne, New Jersey. Circa 1965.

A postcard my father sent me from Israel. 1960's.

James and Rebecca Bjornstad. Circa 1967.

Anthony Collarile and me. Circa 1970.

Bob and Gretchen Passantino. Circa 1974.

My father, Danny, and me in Hawaii. 1977.

My father and me. 1978.

Walter Martin with all six of his children and daughter-in-law, Anne, at home in San Juan Capistrano. Circa 1978.

The Bible Answer Man
Walter Martin and Hank Hanegraaff

Walter Martin defending the orthodox Christian position on *The Phil Donahue Show*. 1980.

Walter Martin and his mentor, Frank Gaebelein. 1981.

My father walking me down the aisle and serving Rick and I communion. August 28, 1982.

Walter Martin and his dear friend, John Warwick Montgomery. 1987.

Rick and I with my father and stepmom, Darlene. 1987.

The Bible Answer Man
Walter Martin and Hank Hanegraaff

5

MORE HEIRLOOM MEMORIES, MADALYN MURRAY O'HAIR, THE OSMOND BROTHERS, AND THE KINGDOM OF THE CULTS

My dad and I often took walks in the beautiful hills near our home. I can still recall him wearing his golf hat (even though he rarely ever played). Our walks together were often consumed with talks about the Lord. A memory that stands out was when he told me to "keep track of God." He encouraged me to start a journal of my prayer requests, record the answers to them, and to read this book whenever I needed to be reminded, more personally, of the goodness of God. He told me this kind of record would encourage my heart, especially in the valleys, and would continuously bless me as I witnessed, first-hand, that God's track record is perfect; the Lord will never fail His children.

A fascinating story my dad shared with me was about a dear friend of his who'd suffered from hiccups on a regular basis. His friend begged God to heal this affliction. The Lord answered his prayer by instructing him to pinch his lip directly beneath his nose as hard as he could stand for one full minute whenever the hiccups came, and they would stop.

When Rick and I raised our four daughters, we taught them to use this remedy when they had hiccups and shared their grandad's unique story with them. It takes a few tries but works if done correctly. We've gone on to tell it to our grandchildren. They all have witnessed the Lord take away their hiccups immediately following this simple instruction.

Our grandson David, when he was a little boy, once heard a child hiccupping in a grocery store. He loudly remarked, "Someone needs to pinch her lip!" While at a garage sale with my three granddaughters — Kayla, Lauren, and Bekkah — we heard two girls complaining they both had hiccups. As I made our purchase, I told them how to make them stop. They followed my instructions and were thrilled when their hiccups stopped; they were amazed to hear how the Lord was a part of that happening. God gives us opportunities to share His love with people at the most unexpected times, in the most unusual places. His timing is supernatural. I doubt those girls will ever forget how the Lord took away their hiccups that day. It also blessed my granddaughters and me to witness this miracle bless people we had just met.

Little did my father realize how a small miracle, the Lord had given his friend more than thirty years ago, would impact the lives of his children, his grandchildren and those in our path. These stories, without a doubt, demonstrate the goodness of God.

I enjoyed sharing my life with my dad, asking his advice, learning more about his life, sharing our burdens, and gaining treasures I carry in my heart to this day. I often played my guitar for him, sharing songs I had written. He loved them so much he told me he wanted to get them published. I enjoyed hearing a beautiful poem about the Lord he'd written and had taken the time to share with me. He was faithful in everything God gave him to do, including the kind of parent he was to his children. I never doubted he would always be there to turn to and that he would love me unconditionally. I loved the different colors of my father. He was the faithful eye on my life, the spiritual mentor, a friend to laugh with, a precious grandfather to the children I later had with my husband Rick, and a great man of God to the entire mission field God had called him to — his family, his friends and the lost. It was fun watching him do the *Bible Answer Man* program from his study in our home in San Juan Capistrano, during our early years there, before CRI had its offices set up in a formal way. Later, as CRI grew, it soon moved to other locations and then to its new international headquarters in Irvine, California.

It was an enormous gift to have my father officiate my wedding ceremony in 1982. It was a tradition in our family for him to perform the marriage ceremonies of his children. I was the third to receive this blessing. To this day, I love listening to his beautiful prayer for Rick and me and his brief comments that followed our vows:

> Eternal God, Our Father, Creator, Preserver of all mankind, Giver of all spiritual grace and author of everlasting life in Jesus Christ: send thy blessing upon these thy children Rick and Cindee, whom we bless in thy name. That they, living faithfully together, may surely perform and keep the vow and covenant between them made whereof this ring given and received is a token and a pledge and may ever remain in perfect love and peace together and that according to

thy law through Jesus Christ our Lord. Amen.

Those whom God hath joined together let no man put asunder. For as much as Rick and Cindee have consented together in holy wedlock and have witnessed the same before God and this company and thereto have given and pledged their promise each to the other that declared the same by giving and receiving a ring and by joining hands, I pronounce that they are husband and wife in the name of the Father and of the Son and of the Holy Spirit. Amen.

God the Father, God the Son, God the Holy Spirit bless, preserve, and keep. The Lord mercifully with His favor look upon you and fill you with all spiritual benediction and grace that you may so live together in this life and in the world, which is to come, you may inherit life everlasting through Jesus Christ our Lord. Amen....

I have the honor of presenting to you, Mr. and Mrs. Rick Morgan.

A brief clip of our wedding can be seen on my Cindee Martin Morgan YouTube channel at
https://www.youtube.com/watch?v=x1xtYyHI2r4&t=43s.

Having an amazing sense of humor, Walter Martin passed out the following message, at my reception, when greeted by our guests. (My stepmom, Darlene, had ordered this humorous message on white business cards for him.) The card said, "I am the Father of the Bride: Nobody's paying much attention to me today, but I can assure you that I am getting my share of attention. The banks and several business firms are watching me very closely."

As God would have it, it was my dear mom who introduced me to the man I would one day marry. Rick had purchased a piano and received a referral to my mother for lessons. While he didn't take piano lessons long, this was how the Lord planned for us to meet. Rick was delighted when he discovered my father was Walter Martin. He had listened to him many times on the *Bible Answer Man* program and greatly valued the ministry of CRI.

During the first year of our marriage, Rick called in to the *Bible Answer Man* program to ask his new father-in-law a "quick question" about predestination, knowing they differed on this issue. My father didn't expect his call and sounded amused. He briefly responded to Rick's question but didn't mention to his listeners he was speaking with his new son-in-law. Right from the start, my dad loved Rick, and they became like father and son.

Rick enjoyed when he had opportunity to drive my father to his Bible class at Newport Mesa, in California. A fond memory of Rick's was my father asking him to hurry, when they were running late, telling him he'd "pay for the ticket." The Lord was merciful; they didn't get one, and I'm sure they both repented! My father did like to drive but also enjoyed when he could relax — something he never had enough time to do in this life.

Rick and I found it intriguing that Walter Martin and his mentor Dr. Barnhouse disagreed on the issue of the sovereignty of God. My father held to the Arminian view of the free will of man—although he did mention to me that he believed that *certain events* in the Bible were predestined (one of his examples was Judas's betrayal of Jesus). Growing up, he taught me the free will view. In my twenties, however, I came to believe as Dr. Barnhouse did. I, too, became a Presbyterian (PCA) after being persuaded first by Scripture, R. C. Sproul's *Tabletalk* magazine, and by my husband Rick. The last theological talk I recall having with my dad was at a Baker's Square restaurant. He was always kind whenever we talked about theology, but I could tell he was a bit frustrated this time, while at the same time he respected my earnest conviction. What I valued in my dad was his willingness to always hear me out. We talked about predestination; I made my case, and he made his, with neither of us giving an inch. He discovered his daughter could be as stubborn as her father when it came to standing firm in a doctrine of which I was convinced. Yet, like his relationship with Dr. Barnhouse, ours would not be hindered by this theological difference. Walter Martin knew that the bond between us was Christ, who is the tie that binds, and refused to divide over what he saw as a secondary issue. This taught me to show more grace to those with whom I disagreed.

Not surprisingly, God gave my father more opportunities to debate Madalyn Murray O'Hair. During a question-and-answer time in his Bible class, he was asked a question about this unforgettable atheist. It was fascinating to hear his commentary and learn more details not commonly known.

> QUESTION: On one of your tapes, you mentioned a five-hour debate you had with Madalyn Murray O'Hair. Are the tapes available?
>
> MARTIN: Madalyn — and I can't quote her because it's obscene — has refused to let me release the tapes even if we pay her a royalty for them. I can understand her reluctance — her clock got cleaned, and she definitely does not want that in the public mind. I did it for five hours on NBC radio, an hour on television, and an hour and a half on NBC radio in Cleveland. So, I actually have seven hours and twenty-five minutes of debate with Madalyn Murray O'Hair, but she will not let me release it. If I were her, I wouldn't let me release it, either, because nothing hurts worse than to be exposed. Once you get through Madalyn's yelling, screaming, and arguing about the

church and get down to her reasons, she hasn't got anything to say, and it became very apparent as we had the lecture.

She got furious at me on NBC. She was swearing by the time we got two-thirds of the way through the program, and it's on the tape. She turned to me when we came to a station break, and she said, "You know what the trouble with you is?" And I said, "I'm sure there are lots of them, Madalyn." She said, "You're too damn smart." And I said, "What do you mean?" She said, "You know what I mean. All this logic and all this stuff you learned. You just throw out this stuff at everybody."

I said, "Right, every chance I get with people like you, because you're dangerous, and you have to be dealt with. Count yourself fortunate. You're only debating me tonight on NBC and *I'm benevolent*. Pray that you never meet John Warwick Montgomery, because if he ever meets you, there will be no mercy whatsoever."

You know what happened? A year and a half later, she debated John Warwick Montgomery in Chicago — and he ate her for breakfast, lunch, and dinner! [The class erupts in laughter.] I mean, I got to feeling sorry for her; he just took her apart. So, that's the difference between Montgomery and myself. You see, I *do* show the quality of mercy, *and I pray to God she'll get saved* — because her son got saved, Bill Murray, and he witnesses to her. Madalyn would be a fearless witness for Christ, *if she gets saved*.[1]

The Lord gave Walter Martin several hours to witness to America's most famous atheist. It's disturbing to recall how Madalyn Murray O'Hair left this world; O'Hair, her youngest son, and her granddaughter were kidnapped and murdered. Madalyn had dedicated her life to opposing the gospel, died a violent death, and now knows there is a God to whom we each must answer. Her eldest son, William J. Murray III, became a Christian. He wrote a book entitled *My Life without God*. He details the nightmare he lived growing up and shares his journey to the Cross.[2] William Murray became a pastor and is the chairman of the Religious Freedom Coalition.[3]

Walter Martin shared many interesting stories with his Bible class about reaching out to those who are unsaved, to encourage the body of Christ. One story he recounted was about a few members of the Osmond family:

---

[1] From a recording of Walter Martin's Bible Study class, July 17, 1983. Copyright Christian Research Institute.
[2] See https://blog.godreports.com/2017/04/son-of-americas-most-famous-atheist-became-a-pastor-recounts-his-mothers-grisly-demise/.
[3] https://religiousfreedomcoalition.org/.

> We learned that some of the Osmond brothers had gotten a hold of my tape "The Maze of Mormonism," had listened to it, and that the repercussions were fantastic. It shook the rafters in the thinking members of the family. Daddy Osmond had to sit down and assure the boys that whatever I was saying couldn't possibly be true. But at least I stirred up such a controversy that they listened to the tape. Isn't that wonderful? *That it got that high.* Don't think that the Word of God — when it's planted — doesn't bring forth fruit, because it does. So, we just praise and thank the Lord for that. Pray for them, because I think they're honest people. There are a lot of honest people in Mormonism. They are just terribly deceived, and we want to pray that the Lord will set them free.[4]

Like millions, I always have appreciated the talents of the Osmond family. Years ago, after reading about some of Marie Osmond's painful trials, I was reminded to pray for this family that needs to know the real Jesus of the Bible. The fact that my father's tape was listened to by some of the Osmond family is yet another reminder that God is in control of every life He's created. They listened to my father's tape, and by doing so, the light of truth was given an opportunity to face off with the darkness they walked in. I don't know if any of the Osmond family has come face-to-face with Jesus, but I am encouraged to know that the Lord used Walter Martin's witness to present to them the real Jesus, bringing the truth to their door.

In 1985, I recall my father excitedly telling me that *Newsweek* magazine had listed *Kingdom of the Cults* as one of ten best-selling spiritual books in America. After telling him I was proud of him, I jokingly told him, "Let another's lips praise thee" (Proverbs 27:2). This drew an enormous grin as he playfully extended his right hand, remarking, "You may kiss my ring." He marveled at the work the Lord was doing in his life and knew he was being used by Him; he gave God the glory.

In spite of his accomplishment, Walter Martin received strong criticism for not classifying the Catholic church as a cult in *The Kingdom of the Cults*. I firmly believe that being raised by a Catholic mother (and graduating from Catholic schools) helped Walter Martin see that the Lord could draw His children from all corners of the Earth, in spite of the errors embraced and often taken to our graves. He taught that the litmus test for a Christian is having a true relationship with Jesus Christ — as revealed in God's Word — that is demonstrated by the fruit of our lives. Walter Martin believed, "For it

---

[4] From a recording of Walter Martin's Bible Study class, May 27, 1984. Copyright Christian Research Institute.

is by grace you have been saved, through faith — and this is not from yourselves, it is the gift of God — not by works, so that no one can boast. For we are God's handiwork, created in Christ Jesus to do good works, which God prepared in advance for us to do" (Ephesians 2:89 NIV). As the Bible says, "For now we see through a glass, darkly, but then face to face" (1 Corinthians 13:12a KJV). The lack of clarity Christians experience has produced error in *both Catholic and Protestant Churches*. Can certain errors cost a man his soul? Absolutely. This is why my father warned against heresy wherever it reared its ugly head. One of the things I admired about him, however, was his ability to identify the biblical common ground he had with many denominations, to build on it, and to expose error, trusting the Lord to bring conviction wherever necessary.

Walter Martin insisted the Catholic Church contained what he called "the core doctrine" of Christianity. *The Kingdom of the Cults* acknowledges this fact when it explains the efforts of the Catholic church to combat the cults. Walter Martin points out, "...the Roman Catholic Church has recently begun detailed research in the area of non-Christian cults and sects, so effective have been the methods of both American-based and indigenous cults in proselytizing Roman Catholic converts."[5] Walter Martin never classified the Catholic church as a cult; he actually mentions *their efforts* to expose them. It is evident he is including them in mainstream Christianity based on the *essential Christian doctrine* in which the historic Catholic church is rooted. He immediately goes on to warn the Christian world about the rise of the cults, giving this admonition based on the exhortation of 2 Timothy 3:16: "...The church must be prepared to defend the claims of Scripture interpreted by the Holy Spirit that it alone is inspired by God and is profitable for doctrine, for reproof, for correction and for instruction in righteousness."[6]

---

[5] *The Kingdom of the Cults*, 358.
[6] *The Kingdom of the Cults*, 358.

6

CATHOLICISM, JOHN ANKERBERG, AND THE TRINITY BROADCASTING NETWORK (TBN)

During a sermon to his Bible class, in 1985, Walter Martin further clarifies his views regarding the Catholic church:

> I think it's very important that we recognize there are differences that do persist. There are Roman Catholics who are true Christians, who love the Lord Jesus Christ and trust Him as their Savior. I believe that they are Christians *not because of the Roman Catholic church* but *despite* the Roman Catholic church and the things which it has added to biblical theology....*It is not the core of Catholicism which disturbs us,* because they confess the Trinity, the deity of Christ, the virgin birth, the perfection of our Lord, His miracles, His vicarious death on the cross, His bodily resurrection, salvation through Him alone, resurrection from the dead, ascension into heaven, our great high priest before the Father after the order of Melchizedek, they believe also in the second coming of Jesus Christ, the establishment of the Kingdom of God on Earth, and they loudly maintain that they have always believed in justification by faith as notes in the current Catholic Bibles indicate. So, they believe in this as well as in eternal judgment and in bliss for the redeemed in heaven. Now, that's the basic outline of Christian theology.... There's no hostility on the part of Protestantism to historic Catholic theology — classic Catholic theology — because in the beginning, there was only one universal

church. The Apostles' Creed clearly states, "I believe in...the holy catholic Church." It does not say *Roman Catholic*. It says catholic, which meant the universal church.[1]

Walter Martin identifies the biblical common ground Protestants have with Catholics while rejecting unbiblical traditions added by men. In this way, he was much like the lay theologian C. S. Lewis, who sought to build bridges to those who embraced what Lewis called "mere Christianity."

My father highly esteemed Lewis and wrote a sequel to his book *Screwtape*, entitled *Screwtape Writes Again*. He dedicated this work to Lewis, stating, "To the memory of C. S. Lewis, a dedicated Christian apologist and evangelist who made insight into the Satanic realm a vital practiced study."[2]

During a question-and-answer time in his Bible class, again Walter Martin was asked if all Catholics are saved. He answered:

> Are Baptists saved? Are Pentecostals saved? Are Methodists saved? Are Episcopalians saved? You're not saved because you belong to any denomination. You're saved if you have a relationship with the Lord Jesus Christ — if you've been born again. And, there are Catholics that are born again. In fact, one of them is going to be speaking for us in June. Doctor, Professor, Father Mitchell Pacwa, whom I debated on *The John Ankerberg Show*, is going to be here, speaking to our Bible class on Sunday. You will find that he is a bearded Jesuit who has a real love for the Lord Jesus and preaches the gospel. You'll get a real kick out of listening to him; I do because we're good friends. He's also working now with Christian Research Institute to get information on the cults for Catholics. He's very interested in getting that kind of information, and we're providing that information for him. So, we thank the Lord for the opportunity to be able to help Catholics escape from the cults.[3]

About seven months later, Walter Martin answered a few questions in his Bible class involving Fr. Pacwa and his ability to defend the Catholic position and whether he was a recognized Catholic theologian.

Walter Martin explained that Mitchell Pacwa "has more credentials than

---

[1] From a recording of Walter Martin's Bible Study class, May 19, 1985. Copyright Christian Research Institute.
[2] Walter Martin, *Screwtape Writes Again* (Santa Ana, CA: Vision House Publishers, 1975).
[3] From a recording of Walter Martin's Bible Study class, February 22, 1987. Copyright Christian Research Institute.

Carter has liver pills." In a lighthearted way, he also adds, "He's bananas in certain areas, but he's a dear brother…And he thinks I'm bananas. The fact is, he's a good Charismatic Catholic, and we pray together." He also stated, "He is one of the most well-trained of the elite Jesuit core on TV, and…yet a sweet brother."[4] Walter Martin invited Fr. Pacwa to be a fill-in guest teacher at his Bible class. Some have claimed Walter Martin believed Catholicism is a cult. His own words speak plainly to the issue, as does his friendship with Fr. Pacwa. In addition, I am quite certain Walter Martin would hardly ask a cultist to teach his Bible class!

After teaching the class, Fr. Pacwa said that my father jokingly remarked to him that he [Fr. Pacwa] had to "hold the folks back with a whip and a chair" because they "all wanted a piece" of him. They laughed heartily about it.

On a side note, I too have been blessed by Catholics who love Jesus Christ. I am honored to be Facebook friends with Father Mitchell Pacwa, Francis Beckwith, and Mariam Ibraheem. Their lives demonstrate their love for Jesus Christ on an ongoing basis.

It was intriguing to obtain some of the back story directly from Fr. Pacwa of the first time God crossed his path with Walter Martin's. (Fr. Pacwa was kind enough to exchange emails with me about this during the time he was in Poland making videos for his network; they were in the process of opening a Polish language channel there.) Walter Martin and Fr. Pacwa had been invited to have a debate on *The John Ankerberg Show*, contrasting what differed about Catholic and Protestant doctrines.

They first met at the Chattanooga Airport after arriving on the same plane and headed to the hotel to prepare for the debate. The following is a fascinating glimpse of what went on when the cameras were rolling and when they were not. Fr. Pacwa stated:

> He introduced himself in a most friendly way and we hit it off right away. We talked in a friendly way before the debates, and he asked to pray with me while we were still in the hotel, before we went to the studios. We both prayed that God's truth be spoken through us, and not long afterward we went to Ankerberg's studio. Once there, we were sent to different rooms, with just some snacks and no dinner before the debate. I was hungry, but I could wait until afterward for some dinner. I do not remember whether your dad's words were kept after the edits, but he stated on tape that he recognized Catholics as fellow Christians, but we were seriously

---

[4] From a recording of Walter Martin's Bible Study class, February 22, 1987. Copyright Christian Research Institute.

wrong about many doctrines and that would be the topic of the debate. The original beginning of the discussion began with Ankerberg asking me, "What should I call you? If I call you 'Father,' that will anger some of my Evangelical friends; if I do not call you Father, that will anger the catholic viewers."

I immediately responded that in Matthew 23:9 ("And call no man your father on earth, for you have one Father, who is in heaven"), our Lord is addressing a Jewish audience familiar with various sects among them. Instead of the term "sect," they spoke of these groups as "houses" — the house of Hillel, the house of Shammai, etc. The heads of these houses or sects were the "fathers" of the houses, and by this command our Lord was forbidding His disciples from establishing themselves as the heads of different sects, much as in 1 Corinthians 1:12–13, 3:21–23, where the Corinthians had divided themselves among Apollos, Paul, and Cephas (Peter) in false divisions that could have developed into sects. Yet, in the same epistle, St. Paul insisted on being known as their father: 1 Corinthians 4:12 "I do not write this to make you ashamed, but to admonish you as my beloved children. For though you have countless guides in Christ, you do not have many fathers. For I became your father in Christ Jesus through the gospel."

Furthermore, St. John addressed a whole group of men in his community as fathers: 1 John 2:13-14 "I am writing to you, fathers, because you know Him who is from the beginning. I am writing to you, young men, because you have overcome the evil one. I write to you, children, because you know the Father. I write to you fathers, because you know Him who is from the beginning. I write to you, young men, because you are strong, and the word of God abides in you, and you have overcome the evil one."

Finally, I told Ankerberg that he had been comfortable in calling your dad "*Dr.* Walter Martin," and the word "doctor" means teacher; why did he accept that title, which our Lord also forbade? (Matthew 23:8 "But you are not to be called rabbi, for you have one teacher, and you are all brethren.") Your dad commented that he liked that discussion very much because it was very informative, and he posed no disagreements.

For the rest of the debates, he did pose plenty of objections, and we went back and forth quite a bit. However, when I saw him again some months later, he was quite upset that Ankerberg's people had edited the debates; he had enjoyed the exchanges, and he did not like the unfairness. For that reason, he invited me as a guest on his radio show so that we could have fairer exchanges, and I appreciated that.

I must admit, the most memorable object in his studio was his stuffed wolf wearing sheepskin. I thought it was hilarious.

We finished the first round of Ankerberg debates well after 11 p.m., and neither of us had eaten yet. We were both getting into a car to get some food and go to our hotel, when John Ankerberg walked up to say farewell. He asked if we could have a word of prayer together, to which I readily agreed.

He began, "Lord let my brother Mitch see the light of truth and leave the Catholic church to become a *true* Christian. Amen." He immediately walked off and got into his car.

Your dad was visibly upset, so I said, "Walter, that wasn't praying; that was debating!"

He responded, "If I were you, I would have prayed right back at him. He deserves it."

However, I responded, "No, Walter. We cannot use prayer as a weapon, so let's pray for him now," which we did rather peacefully. In fact, the only restaurant open was a diner, and all they had left was some cold breakfast cereal. However, we enjoyed each other's company at that simple meal, and the next day we each flew home.

I greatly appreciate Fr. Pacwa's candor about his experience on The John Ankerberg Show and the prayer together that followed between my dad, Ankerberg, and Fr. Pacwa. Knowing my dad, I suspect the reason he told Fr. Pacwa he would have "prayed right back at him [Ankerberg]" was to end on the positive note that they were *all* brothers in Jesus Christ. Fr. Pacwa thought of himself and Walter Martin as being "street punks — he from New York and I from Chicago. We got into it at the debate, fought a clean fight, and ended up as buddies afterward." Fr. Pacwa added, "I maintain my deep respect and love your dad, and I miss him quite a bit. After your father died, I went on radio with Hank and enjoyed those programs very much."

It is evident that Hank has followed in the tradition of my father regarding guests on the *Bible Answer Man* program. Hank has interviewed Protestants, Catholics, and Orthodox Christians. Walter Martin, like many other godly men past and present, considered the Catholic Church to be under the theological umbrella of Christianity. He taught that people in the Catholic Church — who had a genuine relationship with Jesus Christ — were saved in spite of the dangerous heterodoxy he warned existed within its theological walls. He held to this belief throughout his life. I am proud of my father for seeking to sow peace, in love, while standing firm on the truth.

I once accompanied my dad to the set of the Trinity Broadcast Network (TBN) and sat in the studio audience when he was a guest on their *Praise the Lord* program. Jan Crouch announced to the audience that she believed

Walter Martin did not show enough love when he disagreed with the cultist and others. What she failed to understand is that, by telling people the truth (instead of telling them what they want to hear), my father was showing *true* Christian love by not allowing them to walk away without exposing serious theological errors that could cost them their souls.

Although I would have loved to have been there, I was not able to be on the set during what would be Walter Martin's last riveting appearance on TBN. On August 22, 1986, he made many important points that remain relevant to the church today. Here are some brief highlights of that lengthy program, followed by my father's rarely heard comments to his Bible class shortly after he appeared on TBN.

Doug Clark, the host, started off the conversation by stating, "Well, you're Mr. Controversy, you know. You stir up the devil, don't ya?"

[Walter Martin gently responded to this rebuke explaining why the church needs "movers and shakers" who point out error. He emphasized how in order to have a teaching ministry you must teach by contrast and explained that causing controversy, for the sake of the gospel, is necessary.]

MARTIN: Now in the entire history of the church… God raises up apostles, in the beginning prophets, and then the church fathers. Then, after them, the Reformers, and so forth. What was the purpose? It was to bring the church back to the path she deviated from, theologically. Now, we are deviate in a massive way today."

CLARK: When you say *we*, are you talking about the Evangelical?

MARTIN: The Evangelical charismatic church….

[Walter Martin explained how he was invited by churches to teach on various cults and then censored; he was told not to speak about his own expertise and the very reason he was asked to speak. Clark then asked him about a different method of responding to false doctrines and sought my father's opinion on it.]

CLARK: Let me go to another approach for a moment. Matthew, chapter 15: Jesus said about those who taught other doctrines, … "Let them alone" — just preach the truth; it will counteract the error….

MARTIN: Look at your context of Matthew 15. He's not telling you to leave false teachers alone. There were people going around healing in His name, using His name, and so forth. Jesus said, "If they're not against us, they're with us. Leave them alone." But these people *are* against us; they've *declared* against us.

[My father mentions Dave Hunt's book *The Seduction of Christianity*, which was under fire at TBN. He stresses that he and Dave disagree on specific things biblically but wants to discuss an important section of the book where he believes Hunt is correct. Walter Martin quotes Hunt who stressed that all cults believe "that man is or can become a god." He warns that when we teach false doctrine it is evil reminding everyone listening that if you do that, you should be held accountable. Clark wholeheartedly appears to agree with Walter Martin and offers the following Scriptural admonition in Galatians 1: "Even if an angel from heaven come[s] and preach[es] any other gospel to you, let him be accursed."]

[Walter Martin goes on to explain that Copeland and Kenneth Hagen are the ones who are teaching heresy. He emphasizes how people don't want to use names because they don't want to offend people. My father reminds everyone that Paul openly rebuked Hymenaeus and Philetus for not speaking the truth when they taught that the resurrection was past. He wisely mentions how Paul also called out Alexander the coppersmith.]

CLARK: Let me ask you a question, then, about the names you've just named. Do you believe these men are conscientious Christians?

MARTIN: Yep...Doctrinal error.

[Walter Martin urges people to contact those caught in doctrinal error and to confront them in love. He carefully explains that Mormon theology teaches you can become a god and infers this doctrine has crept into the church. At this juncture, he drops a truth bomb as Clark visibly squirms in his chair. He directly quoted Kenneth Copeland which proved the doctrinal error Copeland was teaching. Clark agreed it was error and urged people to not throw out everything someone teaches because they made a mistake. My father stressed how teachers, including himself, are accountable to the Lord.]

MARTIN: We are under authority to holy Scripture. [*applause*] And, if we are teaching this stuff, we should be corrected. And we should not do it anymore.

CLARK: ...Well, it's kind of like a Martin Luther nailing the 95 Theses to the door to purify the doctrine of the church.

MARTIN: And then they nail *you* to the door.

[Clark reminds my father that is the price apologists must pay for trying to "purify" the doctrine. He points out how God raises up men to be salt and light theologically but emphasizes how some may *not* agree with Walter Martin's views. Clark credits Paul Crouch for inviting him back on the program.]

[Walter Martin carefully explains that Paul Crouch answered a letter asking whether he believed men can become gods. While demonstrating a good sense of humor, Clark was sweating bullets. My father quickly read Crouch's response. Much to Clark's relief, it stated that TBN does *not* believe we are gods. Clark wraps up this controversial interview overjoyed by Crouch's response to this question. My father ends this historically powerful discussion with the following righteous declaration.]

MARTIN: "I am telling the truth. God help me," as Luther said, "I can do nothing else."[5]

TBN wasn't happy about many of Walter Martin's comments on their network that night. It didn't gain him brownie points to correct a couple of the health and wealth gospel teachers they supported. He was never invited back on this program. This full interview is widely available on various public venues. Interestingly enough, Walter Martin did not call professing Christians Kenneth Copeland and Kenneth Hagen apostate or heretics, a fact that is surprising to some, yet seems wise to others. He believed in confronting people, in love; he sought them out (first privately) in efforts to show them their doctrinal error(s). He believed in extending to others mercy and forbearance, whenever possible. He gave people the opportunity to dialogue with him in the hope they would turn from teaching that is contrary to the Word of God. That is biblical love. While some teachers immediately would have branded these two prosperity gospel teachers apostate, and then washed their hands of them, Walter Martin was quick to try to help Copeland and Hagan see their error *in the hope and prayer that they would repent.*

He went out of his comfort zone and fought for people. He was never quick to give up on those who claimed to be a brother or sister in Christ. He viewed this mistake, initially, as a doctrinal error that must be repented of, and he gave the benefit of the doubt — regarding a person's salvation — if they claimed to know the real Jesus of the Bible. He never presumed to know the mind of God as to who was saved, in these situations, and who may very well be lost.

My dad was mindful of the fact that people can get confused and misled, but it may not mean they will not ultimately repent with the help of other believers and the Holy Spirit. As James exhorts us, "Let him know that whoever brings back a sinner from his wandering will save his soul from death and will cover a multitude of sins" (James 5:20 ESV). We are supposed to fight for one another, not throw each other away. The Lord instructs us to let the wheat grow with the tares (Matthew 13:30). Walter Martin saw a biblical order to things, and he abided by it. He believed that, in the end, it was God's job to sort out the wheat from the tares, but until that time, God may not be finished yet. He taught me this. If there was no repentance, however, after biblical steps were exhausted, Walter Martin would continue

---

[5] Cindee Martin Morgan, "1/2 Walter Martin/TBN (Trinity Broadcasting Network) 1-2" YouTube video, 23:54, published July 17, 2011, https://www.youtube.com/watch?v=l8xAVR1sG0I; Cindee Martin Morgan, "2/2 Walter Martin/TBN (Trinity Broadcasting Network) Part 2 of 2," YouTube video, 18:40, published July 19, 2011, https://m.youtube.com/watch?v=6eg4Mb_oSQo.

to follow the admonitions of Scripture in response to false teachers who claimed to know Christ. While some may not agree with him, this is how he conducted himself in the body of Christ.

About two weeks after Walter Martin was on TBN's *Praise the Lord* program, he shared with his Bible class that Paul Crouch had corrected a stated belief of his that was theologically wrong. A different statement made by Crouch, however, had been heard by someone else, and it was brought to my father's attention. My father had not been aware of Crouch's statement before appearing on TBN. Here are some of the colorful highlights from Walter Martin's Bible class on September 7, 1986, discussing his last TBN appearance:

> Now, I have an announcement to make. On TBN I stated that Paul Crouch had written a letter stating that TBN does not teach or believe that man may become a god. I have to correct that. As of July 17, of this year, on tape Paul Crouch said, quote, "I am a god." If you're listening, Paul, since I can't get to you, *you are not a god*. You will never be a god. You are an embryo Mormon. Right now. Your theology is corrupt, and it's dangerous to the body of Christ. It originated with the Mormons and is carried on now by Kenneth Copeland, and now broadcast over the TBN network. It is heretical. It is false doctrine. It is cultic. You have crossed the line. It is now necessary for the Christian church to take disciplinary action, and if the Christians won't do it, you have nobody to blame but yourselves. If you tolerate evil at the heart of the church, you become an accessory after the fact of the crime. So, if you remain silent, you become as guilty as the people who are doing it. That's a terrible indictment, but that's Scripture. So, I'm doing what Ezekiel said to do. The Watchman is supposed to make lots of noise so the city will wake up. Isn't that right? Well, the Watchman is going to make noise, lots of it, on the *Bible Answer Man* program and on secular television. If they're not going to correct this theology and stop Kenneth Copeland and these other people from teaching Mormon doctrine on TBN, Christians should stop, en masse, supporting TBN.
>
> I will make a copy of the tape available so that you can hear it for yourselves. We're trying to get a video copy, only you can't get documentation out of TBN. TBN thinks I have spies all over the place. I don't. [*audience laughs*] People keep sending me information; I don't ask for it. A lady sent me information — a letter from TBN — saying that because I rehashed Dave Hunt and his book, that's the reason why they didn't replay it [my father's last TBN appearance]. Rehash it? They've been attacking Hunt and his book

'round the clock. Doug Clark said I'm Mr. Controversy. I didn't make myself Mr. Controversy. I became controversial for one reason: I spoke out, and the minute you speak out on evil, you become controversial. If you don't speak out on evil, then you're a wimp. I've never been accused of that. [*audience laughs*] So, write TBN. Write in and say, "Is Paul Crouch a god?" Imagine all these years you've been worshipping the wrong person. [*audience laughs*] Is he a god? I wonder if Jan would tell us how the god acts at home.

It's like Roy Masters debating Jon Stewart one time, and Roy Masters was asked by Jon Stewart, "Are you sinless?"

And he said, "Of course I am. I'm perfect."

So, Jon Stewart — a good lawyer — said, "Your wife's out there. Can she come to the microphone for a minute?"

He brought Mrs. Masters in there and said, "Is *he* perfect?"

"Well, uh, sometimes he gets angry," she replied.

"Oh, then, he's not perfect," Jon announced, and Masters died on the microphone. What could he say? His wife was there. If your wife doesn't know what you're like, I mean, don't ever tell your wife you're a god. [*audience laughs*] Oh boy, that is one fallen idol, kid. Right there.

Can you see the arrogance and the egotism that's behind this — for a lost sinner saved by grace to claim to be a deity? I mean, how far out can you get? So far out you can't get an orbital fix on you.[6]

Walter Martin came down hard on Paul Crouch, but it was appropriate. Paul was teaching doctrine that was dangerous and, worse yet, it appeared he was being deceptive about it. Walter Martin initially took Paul Crouch at his word until the evidence revealed that Paul said he believed that he (Paul) *is* a god. Paul persisted in teaching false doctrine.

Over a year later, on November 15, 1987, Walter Martin told his Bible class during question-and-answer time, "I've already delivered myself on this subject, to Paul personally, so I'm not telling tales out of school....He is fomenting, promoting, and distributing heretical false theology and he does it regularly, and he knows better. I say this publicly."

Did Paul ever contact my father and renounce his doctrinal errors? He did not. For Paul's sake, I hope that before he stood face-to-face with the one and only God, he repented of them. Walter Martin was salt and light to Paul Crouch, Kenneth Hagan, and Kenneth Copeland while warning the church to be careful of their false teaching. There is no other God apart from

---

[6] From a recording of Walter Martin's Bible Study class, September 7, 1986. Copyright Christian Research Institute.

the God of the Bible. The Old Testament says in Deuteronomy 4:35, "Unto thee it was shewed, that thou mightest know that the LORD He is God; there is none else beside Him."

The New Testament also affirms in John 17:3, "And this is life eternal, that they might know Thee the only true God, and Jesus Christ, whom Thou hast sent." And then in 1 Timothy 2:5: "For there is one God, and one mediator between God and men, the man Christ Jesus."

7

FINAL DAYS AND WITNESSING TO MUHAMMAD ALI

The grandfatherly side of Walter Martin was something to behold. While visiting Rick, our girls, and me in Arizona (after the birth of our third daughter), he was asked by a radio host his reason for being in Arizona. He joyfully took the opportunity to announce the birth of his fifth granddaughter, Richelle, during that KFLR program on Family Life Radio. Here is a brief excerpt:

HOST/ GEORGE: And today at Midway, we're going to talk about cults. We'll talk about, I suppose we'll go all the way from the New Age movement all the way back to other cults that have been around for years and years. We'll talk about perhaps the Moonies — why we don't hear as much about them — or what's happening with the Moonies in 1988. We're very privileged to have Dr. Walter Martin from the Christian Research Institute live with us, in studio, and welcome to KFLR, Dr. Martin.

WALTER MARTIN: Hi, George, nice to be here with you.

GEORGE: Appreciate you stopping by. Your reason for being here, in the valley, is kind of an exciting personal one. Maybe you could share that with us first before we get down to some of the business at hand.

MARTIN: Yes, for a change, I'm not speaking. I'm not recording. I'm not doing a seminar. I'm not preaching in a church. I'm here to celebrate the birth of my newest granddaughter, Richelle Morgan.

GEORGE: That is neat. How many does that make now, that you have?

MARTIN: Five, but I'm very young. I mean, don't get the wrong idea. [*laughs*]

GEORGE: Well, congratulations, and we wish you and your children and your grandchildren very well. So, your son and daughter live here in the valley, needless to say.

MARTIN: Yes, my daughter lives here with her husband, and my other son, too [Danny].

GEORGE: Oh, so they both live out here.

MARTIN: Yeah.

GEORGE: And you live out there on the West Coast.

MARTIN: Yes, well, if Nostradamus is right, you're going to have beachfront property here. [*laughs*]

GEORGE: Now, that wouldn't happen to be why you're here?

MARTIN: No, no nothing to do with that. [*laughs*][1]

During the time my dad and stepmom were visiting us, he had to do a *Bible Answer Man* program from our house. Our pastor at the time, Bill Phillips, asked if he could come over and listen to Walter Martin on the air. We told him to please feel welcome to come. My father wasn't feeling well but decided to do the program anyway. So, while our pastor sat across from him in a chair, Walter Martin did the *Bible Answer Man* program *lying down* with pillows underneath his feet. He didn't miss a beat. Our pastor was thrilled to meet him and to be there. It made him chuckle to see that Walter Martin was quite the trouper. Come rain or shine, he professed the gospel of Jesus Christ.

Walter Martin was comfortable in his own skin. (I married a man like that, but I have never possessed that level of confidence.) My dad once told me he was late getting to CRI to do a *Bible Answer Man* program when an unexpected thing happened. He ran through the parking lot, ran through the building, ran down the hall to his office, jumped in his chair, and then it broke beneath him. The Bible Answer Man hit the floor about one second before show time. With his feet straight up in the air, he said to his first caller, "This is Walter Martin. You're on the air!" He sat like that, answering questions, until the first break. It took a lot to rattle my dad. His ministry, and raising six children, had produced nerves of steel.

In 1988, CRI moved into its new international headquarters building in Irvine, California. My father drove my husband and our young daughters there to show us what the Lord had done for CRI (just as he had done with me when I was a little girl). I'll never forget him looking at me, when we had a moment alone, and stretching out his arms as he exclaimed, "Cindee, this

---

[1] Originally aired May 10, 1988, on KFLR radio. Cindee Martin Morgan, "Walter Martin Announces the Birth of His 5th Granddaughter, Richelle Morgan," YouTube video, 2:06, published May 31, 2009, https://www.youtube.com/watch?v=qfjE7r_T9lw.

is my dream!" He marveled at the way the Lord had raised up this extraordinary apologetics ministry and was honored God used him to do it. I was deeply moved to have the opportunity to share this precious moment in time with my father.

During the final three weeks I would have with my dad in this life, he mentioned how sad he was that he would not be able to see his grandchildren grow up. This would be the only clue I had, in May of 1989, that he was contemplating his own death. I was unable, at the age of twenty-eight, to process the prospect of losing him. I remember thinking he *had* to be mistaken, so I said a word of encouragement to him and told him a lighthearted joke to try to lift his spirits. What I wasn't aware of was that *he already knew* his health was rapidly declining. He was a severe diabetic, like his father, and the disease had taken a dramatic toll on his heart. But my dad looked healthy and was active in ministry, and I couldn't imagine a world without him in it. He also had just published his last book, *The New Age Cult*, a work that evaluated and examined some of the major tenants of the New Age movement.

Only nine days before the Lord called him home, Walter Martin delivered his last seminar on June 17, 1989, at Arrowhead Springs Christian Conference Center for a small pastors' conference. His sermon was entitled, "The Way to Holiness." A video created by a YouTube friend, who is known as GMDOCNICE, features most of the audio recording. Here are some highlights of my father's final message to the church:

> "Fight the good fight of faith! Take hold of eternal life where unto thou are also summoned and have professed a good profession before many witnesses. I give thee this charge in the sight of God who makes all things alive and before Christ Jesus who in the presence of Pontius Pilate witnessed a good confession. Keep this command without spot, unrebukable, until the appearing of our Lord Jesus Christ, who alone possesses immortality dwelling in the light which no man can approach, unto whom no man hath seen nor can see. To Him, honor and power everlasting, Amen."
>
> Notice something here? Linked with holiness, as a byproduct, is fighting the good fight of faith. In other words, the brother who was up here before me was talking about spiritual warfare. There can be no holiness without spiritual warfare. There can be no holiness without spiritual war. You think God is going to give you the fruits of holiness by osmosis? Do you think that after others have sailed through bloody seas, unbelievable conflicts, great controversy, persecution, suffering — even unto death — that you can manifest the holiness of God in your life without conflict? That's madness.

That's what too many Christians are trying to get today. (*applause*) They're trying to get holiness as if you could buy it at Kmart. They're trying to get holiness by running off to deeper-life conferences. They're trying to get holiness by going to hear this evangelist or that evangelist or this TV speaker or this Bible teacher. For God's sake, don't try to get holiness from Walter Martin, because Walter Martin's holiness is borrowed from Jesus Christ! I'm not here for that purpose. I'm here to draw attention to the basic bottom line of what it all means. And the bottom line is that you've got to translate the word *holiness* and *sanctification* and *godliness* into its basic meaning — god likeness: to be like Him, to see Him as He is. That's the joy of the Christian. That's the goal of the Christian. Looking for that blessed hope, the appearing of the glory of the great God and of our Savior Jesus Christ who shall transform these bodies which humiliate us, so that they shall become like unto His own glorious body through that power whereby He is able to subdue everything unto Himself.

So, the good fight of faith is a byproduct of Christ living in you. There is such a thing as spiritual war. And there is such a thing as righteous indignation and godly anger. It is right to be angry in the presence of evil. I will repeat that. It is right, in the sight of God, to be angry in the presence of evil. I am one of God's last angry men. I get in trouble more often than anybody else. The *Bible Answer Man* program indicates that, where I'm often sworn at on the air — for doing nothing other than telling them the truth. They get mad. But the ministry is not a popularity contest. The Christian life is not a popularity contest. You're not here to be popular. You're here to serve. If God happens to give you the love of others and popularity along with it, consider yourself extremely fortunate, but it's not necessary. You can live without it!

Now, this spiritual warfare takes place in the life of the believer when the believer is provoked by evil. If you read Acts chapter 17, you'll find that when Paul was in Athens, waiting for his cohorts, he was provoked by the idolatry which he saw all around him. Remember? When he saw the whole city given over to idolatry, his spirit was provoked! He became angry and he went down and stood in the marketplace by the Temple of Vulcan, where I have stood. Today — still there, right where he was, and, boy, he chewed the Athenians out from top to bottom. It didn't take him very long to do it. By the time he got finished, he had people getting saved, right up on the judgment throne under the Acropolis. They were coming to Christ. Why? Because he told it like it was. Do you know what the

Christian church needs today? It needs men with the guts to tell it like it is. [*applause*]

...I was passing through an airport one time, and as I went through, I looked over, and Muhammad Ali was sitting there. I said, Ah, an opportunity! [*audience laughs*] So, I walked over to him, and I said, "Mr. Ali."

He said, "Yes."

I said, "I don't want your autograph, and I'm not here to bother you. I'm not a celebrity hound," and he laughed. And I said, "We have a mutual friend."

He said, "Who is that?"

I said, "Rocky Marciano. He was a personal friend of mine for many years."

He said, "You know Rocky?"

I said, "Very well. He told me all about his computer fight with you, and all the rest of the things that you did."

He said, "Yes, we had a terrific time. We only used body punches." And he said, "We fought one-minute rounds."

I said, "Well, what did you think of him?" I thought, well, talk about something Ali wanted to talk about, which is fighting, and then when his guard is down, sock it to him! [*audience laughs*] So, I'm a boxing enthusiast who boxed myself and wrestled. So, I was interested, and I recounted the fights to him and the different fights that he had, and so forth.

He said, "Yes, yes."

I said, "What did you think of Marciano? I understand that he was the hardest puncher ever recorded in the history of boxing. He could take you out with a left hand, or a right hand, and never had to travel more than six inches. All he had to do was get one clean shot at you."

He said, "It's true." He said, "We only hit each other from the shoulders down. That man hit so hard with sixteen-inch gloves on — not standard gloves — sixteen-inch gloves. He hit so hard with sixteen-inch gloves that my arms were paralyzed, and my ribs were bruised for six weeks." He said, "If he had had on standard gloves and he could of got a shot at me, woo-e! I was on the bicycle and moving away as fast as I could." He said, "Hit so hard it was like getting hit with a fist full of rocks!" He said, "They called him Rocky rightly."

So, we talked a few minutes more, and he had a little book there. A Mohammedan book, an Islamic book. And he said to me, "Ah, I've been reading this stuff here. You believe in hell?" The man's terrified of hell, because he knows he's going there.

And I said to him, "Well, Ali," I said, "the greatest man that ever lived, Jesus Christ, said there was a hell, and He preached on it more times than He ever preached on heaven."

He said, "No [Stated with dread]."

I said, "Yes. And, Jesus always told the truth."

He said, "Yeah."

I said, "There is a hell." I had a chance to witness to him, but nevertheless, he was attracted in our conversation first by the material, our mutual interest, and then the spiritual. I had my cross on. People say, why do you wear such a big cross? Just for that reason. It attracts attention. Secondly, I found out devils don't like it, and what they don't like, I wear. [*applause*]...What was it that shook up Mohammed Ali? It was the fact that he was encountering the truth of Jesus Christ, right there, and he was seeing Christ in me! I know that's true. I know because others have told me exactly the same thing, and I'm not alone. Every single time you open your mouth and you can't remember what you're saying afterwards, it's God the Holy Spirit that's confronting those people. He's bringing them the conviction of sin and righteousness and judgment. There is such a thing as righteous indignation. I said it before, and I want to say it again. If you don't become indignant in the presence of evil, there is something wrong with your godlikeness! If you can sit still in the middle of pornography, filthy language, depravity — if you can sit still in the midst of people mocking Christ or Christianity — if you can sit still and never say anything, I challenge very much whether the image of God lives in you! Because he that is born of God does not practice sin as a habit. He not only knows God, but His seed remains within him. And it's going to come out in his life and in his witness.

...So, there is such a thing as spiritual warfare, and I want to close with this emphasis because it fits in with the life of holiness. Those that are holy will sanctify the Lord God in their hearts. They will give to people that ask them a reason for the hope that lies within them. They will fight the good fight of faith. They will lay hold on eternal life. They will not sit still or be silent in the presence of evil. The bottom line of holiness is action in obedience to the power of Christ. In 2 Corinthians chapter 10, we are told that we are at spiritual conflict. The weapons of our warfare are not carnal but mighty from God to the pulling down of strongholds! Right? To the demolishing of arguments, and every proud thing that exalts itself against the knowledge of God — that's war — and taking into captivity every thought to the person of Jesus Christ.

In the words of a great old hymn, I close. We don't sing it much anymore. We sing a lot of choruses. We sing a lot of music, which unfortunately sounds so much alike, but only the words change, and the music stays the same. I'm a little tired of that. I like to go back to some of the great old hymns of the church. And, I'll close with one of them:

> "Rise up, O men of God!
> Have done with lesser things;
> Give heart and soul and mind and strength
> To serve the King of Kings.
>
> ...Rise up, O men of God!
> The church for you doth wait,
> Her strength unequal to her task;
> Rise up and make her great!"

He that has ears to ear, hear what the Spirit says to the church. Obey Him! Obedience is better than sacrifice. Amen.[2]

---

[2] GMDOCNICE, "2012 Message to Christians – Fight the Good Fight of Faith," YouTube video, 16:23, published January 1, 2012, https://www.youtube.com/watch?v=dRWz58Nyahw.

8

"IT WAS SEA AND ISLANDS NOW; THE GREAT CONTINENT HAD SUNK LIKE ATLANTIS." – C. S. LEWIS

Rick, our girls, and I had just moved, from Arizona to Minnesota. I was hesitant to leave Arizona because I enjoyed the fact it was only a seven-hour drive to my dad's home in San Juan Capistrano. He assured me, however, that he would visit often.

Not yet having a home of our own, we were invited to live with my sister Jill and our brother-in-law, Kevin, while we began the search. They graciously put up with our family the four months prior to our finding our first Minnesota house. They had a large home and were happy to allow us to live there and share expenses. We were excited to be with them and to live in a state with gorgeous seasons. Having moved from Glendale, Arizona (a place that only knows how to do spring and summer), it was refreshing. Kevin and Jill were fun tour guides. We went everywhere together and had a wonderful time.

Early the morning of June 26, we received a call from my sister Elaine, in California. Rick had already left for work. Our father was gone — he was with the Lord. My brother, Danny, also living in Minnesota, came over to the house as we began facing a loss difficult to accept. I'll never forget the comments of our two oldest daughters trying to comfort their devastated mom. Stacie, then six, said, "Don't worry, Mommy, you might be with him sooner than you think." Our daughter, Sharon, then four — who has her Grandad Martin's hilarious sense of humor — joked, "Did Grandad *beat us to die?* Get it? He had diabetes; he *beat us to die!*" Laughter helps you heal. The

Lord has countless ways to comfort His children — oftentimes, through our own.

About two months prior to our move to Minnesota, Rick, the girls, and me had spent three weeks with my father at his home in California. The visit ended not long before his death. The blessing of the Lord's timing of this is not lost on us. I quietly cried the entire flight to California as we traveled there for my father's funeral. I was headed to my dad's house, a place he would never live again. I felt like I was five again, not knowing how to process the deepest loss I'd ever known. The grief seemed unbearable. I remember tearfully explaining to a kind and concerned flight attendant that I would be OK and, of course, I had to tell her how wonderful my dad was. I explained to this perfect stranger how I had tried not to tell friends about the public side of his ministry because I (mistakenly) thought it would be prideful, but now I needed to tell anyone who would listen how proud I was of him, and still am. I felt much like C. S. Lewis, when he wrote about the loss of his mother: "It was sea and islands now; the great continent had sunk like Atlantis."

This is what grief does; it moves into the heart, uninvited, and breaks it into countless pieces that only God can put back together again. I can testify to the truth — God does that. It doesn't seem possible when you are suffering, but piece by piece God puts us back together again. When we got off the plane at the John Wayne Airport, my brother Bryan, his wife Anne, their two young daughters Amber and Robin, and my sister Elaine met us at the gate. The look on their faces mirrored our own as we hugged one another and cried. We all headed to my father's house in San Juan Capistrano.

The private funeral for my dad was a day that seemed to move in slow motion. Danny and I walked in to the funeral home, together, and soon saw him — off in the distance — peacefully laid out in his coffin. Arm in arm, we made our way to him. I had never seen Danny more torn up. Our father looked better than anyone we'd ever seen in death; he looked alive. He used to joke about leaving instructions for his casket to be delivered late to his funeral because he had been late for most everything else in his life. (I confess I take after him that way.) Recalling his sense of humor always seemed to help, especially in moments like this.

It soon came time to close the casket, and for our family to say our goodbyes. Our daughter Sharon — who'd not shown *any* sign of grief to this point — gazed down at my dad's face from her daddy's arms and cried out in sorrow, "Oh, Grandad!" We had wondered if Sharon was just too young to process this loss. She was processing it.

My father called his grandchildren his grandbunnies. He was an exceptional grandfather who even babysat once for our daughter Stacie's Cabbage Patch doll. I'll never forget walking into the family room one evening and seeing it perched right next to him. He had his arm around the doll; it was quite the sight. My dad looked up at me with a grin and informed me that Stacie had asked him to babysit while she went shopping. I grabbed my camera and took a picture; I had to capture this sweet moment in time. After my father's death, Rick painted a portrait, from the photo, for our family to enjoy and to give to Stacie when she was grown.

One of the greatest comforts the Lord gave our family was when Darlene put the *Bible Answer Man* program on and played it through the speaker system after Walter Martin's funeral so we could hear it throughout the house. People called in to the program to give tributes to Walter Martin, and many were sobbing. A tidal wave of tears mingled with our own as we heard their heartfelt comments. If you are someone who called the program during that time, and are reading this now, thank you; the Lord used you to help us survive our loss. With tributes bouncing off every wall of my father's earthly home, I suddenly could not find my younger sister, Elaine. I eventually discovered her in her room, sitting on her bed softly crying. I hugged her close and took her hand in mine. The intensity of the loss we felt made even breathing seem a chore. Hearing the tributes playing in the distance, I sang her some of the words to a song I love by Joni Erikson Tada, *Joni's Waltz*. "Heaven is nearer to me. At times it is all I can see. Sweet music I hear coming down to my ears and I know that it's playing for me. For I am Christ my Savior's own bride and redeemed I shall stand by His side. He will say shall we dance, and our endless romance will be worth all the tears I have cried."[1] We felt the Lord's presence as He comforted our hearts.

I must confess that I accidentally wore my dress backward to my father's funeral. The Lord was merciful: it was solid black and extremely plain, making it hard to distinguish the back from the front, which is most likely why I didn't notice until we were back home again. I immediately told my Aunt Gladys about this wardrobe malfunction. Still as beautiful as she was on the *Bride and Groom* show decades before, she hugged me, smiled, and softly said, "Don't worry, honey. I sprayed orange blossom air freshener all over my hair, thinking it was hairspray!" I looked at her more carefully and could see a light mist covering it; suddenly I could smell the orange blossoms. She had generously sprayed her hair only minutes before leaving the powder room. We both laughed, and cried, thinking how amused my dad would be if he saw us at that moment.

He would have also chuckled, that day, to hear his addled sister, Betsy, telling everyone she'd raided the maid's cart at the hotel she and her son were staying at. Aunt Betsy would then zip open her Mary Poppins–type purse to

---

[1] Joni Eareckson, "Joni's Waltz," track 8 on *Joni's Song*, Word, 1981, vinyl LP album.

proudly show off her shampoos, conditioners, and little bars of soap. While we were visiting in the kitchen, Aunt Betsy strolled in and casually walked over to the poppyseed lemon muffins sitting on the counter. She grabbed one, and demanded to know, "What are these *black dots* in these muffins?! They look like those ticks that cause Lyme disease!" We burst into laughter, which is so good for the soul, especially following a funeral. Aunt Betsy laughed, too, blissfully unaware of her illness. She could navigate better than anyone I knew in her condition. We loved Aunt Betsy. My father once told me — when I asked him who his favorite sister was — that although he was close to the three of them, Betsy was his favorite because of her sense of humor. He mentioned that my sense of humor reminded him of hers. I smiled but told him I was afraid of the compliment, and hoped I was never in my dear Aunt Betsy's shoes. He smiled back; I suspect that inwardly he, too, prayed his mind stayed intact. God answered his prayer. He spared my dad and our family that type of trial.

Hank Hanegraaff, whom Walter Martin positioned to lead CRI, planned a beautiful memorial service for Walter Martin. Hank was the executive vice president when CRI faced the death of its founder. Our family was comforted by these beautiful tributes included in the bulletin at the service:

"His insightful mind, his forceful logic and his dedication to Orthodox Christianity were seldom, if ever, equaled in the field of contemporary cults."
—Dr. Norman Geisler

"He was a man of surpassing love for Christ, His Word and His people. He ever manifested unswerving fidelity to the essentials of the Christian faith. We served together, laughed together, and prayed together."
—Dr. Desmond Ford

"He was a strong soldier of the cross, a clear-thinking defender of Christianity, and an able expositor of Scripture. He was, to many of us, however, more than a courageous conqueror...He was a loyal friend 'in season and out of season.'"
—Chuck Swindoll

"He was an intrepid warrior for the cause of Christ. He was not afraid to take on any heretic or cultist of any sort."
—Dr. D. James Kennedy

"A true Champion of the Orthodox faith, Dr. Martin was thorough in battling the Occult and the growing number of Cults in our generation. He dealt with people of various faiths in a truthful manner, pointing out their logical and spiritual errors with a Pastor's heart. In an era of diluted faith and obscured thinking, Dr. Martin was a voice constantly calling us back to the bedrock of Christ and the holiness of the Scriptures."

—Dr. James. C. Dobson

"Dr. Martin was a friend and a co-laborer, one of the church's greatest spokesman for sound biblical doctrine."

—Chuck Smith

There were many moving tributes during Walter Martin's service. My brother Bryan was the first in our family to honor our father. Before Bryan was married, he used to travel some with him, for ministry purposes, and would manage his book and tape table. He also did this for our father at Melodyland, during Walter Martin's Bible class. The following are highlights of Bryan's tribute at our dad's memorial service:

> I know that my dad's life and ministry touched many of you here tonight. He was given a commission, by God, to go and preach the gospel. He often said his role was to give every man an answer, a reason for the hope that lies within us, with reverence and humility, from 1 Peter 3:15. We viewed our dad as a spiritual warrior who was sent by God to fulfill the calling of the Scripture.
>
> Dad loved all of us very much, and each of the members of my family felt that love, but he also had a love and a burden for those who needed to know Christ as their Lord and Savior; his life was dedicated to this task. Each of us here tonight will remember Dad and the example that he set for us *to help equip us* for the defense of the gospel. I know many of you are here tonight as a direct result of his ministry — from helping you in how to witness to the cults, to how to defend the gospel, to maybe even coming to know Christ through his ministry. That was Dad's greatest joy, to know that there would be souls saved and be in heaven someday as a result of him sharing the gospel.
>
> He would often tell us stories of people who had come up to him at meetings, or in his Bible class, and share with him about his tapes and books and teaching; his teaching had a tremendous impact on their lives. He was so excited about sharing these stories with us. What I remember most was how he told me that all the praise and the glory would go to Jesus. He did not want to take the credit. It was and is the Holy Spirit who brings people unto salvation. He always emphasized that to me…Dad fought the good fight and we know he is at peace, where he longed to be. As Paul wrote, "I long

to be with Christ which is far better."

All of us will miss him and all of the love and encouragement he brought to us, but I know Dad would want all of us to press on for the cause of the gospel.

Bryan closed by quoting a hymn:

"Stand Up! Stand Up for Jesus"

Stand up! Stand up for Jesus!
  Ye soldiers of the cross;
Lift high His royal banner,
  It must not suffer loss:
From vict'ry unto vict'ry
  His army shall He lead,
Till every foe is vanquished
  And Christ is Lord indeed.

Stand up! Stand up for Jesus!
  The trumpet call obey;
Forth to the mighty conflict
  In this His glorious day.
Ye that are men, now serve Him
  Against unnumbered foes;
'Til courage rise with danger.
  And strength to strength oppose.

Stand up! Stand up for Jesus!
  Stand in His strength alone;
The arm of flesh will fail you;
  Ye dare not trust your own.
Put on the Gospel armor,
  Each piece put on with prayer,
Where duty calls, or danger,
  Be never wanting there.

Stand up! Stand up for Jesus!
  The strife will not be long:
This day the noise of battle,

The next the victor's song;
To him that overcometh
A crown of life shall be;

He, with the King of glory,
Shall reign eternally!

My brother Danny shared a profound poem he'd read at our father's funeral. (Both of my brother's tributes, along with others, can be heard on our WalterMartinJude3 YouTube channel.)

"Safely Home"

I am home in Heaven, dear ones;
Oh, so happy and so bright!
There is perfect joy and beauty
In this everlasting light.

All the pain and grief is over,
Every restless tossing passed;
I am now at peace forever,
Safely home in Heaven at last.

Did you wonder why I so calmly
Trod the valley of the shade?
Oh! But Jesus' love illumined
Every dark and fearful glade.

And He came Himself to meet me
In that way so hard to tread;
And with Jesus' arm to lean on,
Could I have one doubt or dread?

Then you must not grieve so sorely,
For I love you dearly still;
Try to look beyond earth's shadows,
Pray to trust our Father's will.

There is work still waiting for you,
So you must not idly stand;
Do it now, while life remaineth
You shall rest in Jesus' land.

> When the work is all completed,
> He will gently call you home;
> Oh, the rapture of that meeting,
> Oh, the joy to see you come![2]

My husband's tribute was especially memorable to me. He mentioned a time we had picked my dad up from somewhere, and I had hopped in the back to allow my dad to sit in the front with Rick. Knowing they differed on a certain theological position, I asked my dad about it, wanting to hear them discuss it. Rick's heart about stopped, having to theologically go toe-to-toe with the *Bible Answer Man*, but he did manage to get some words out. Suffice it to say, it was a great discussion.[3]

Longtime board member Everett Jacobson also gave a moving tribute, sharing how he comforted my father during a time he was going through a severe personal trial.[4]

When the public memorial service ended, the Martin family was asked to stand in front of the church so that people could meet us, comfort us, and be comforted. Several hundred people formed a line to greet us. We'd never been hugged that many times in our lives; their tears fell with our own. I love and miss my father, but I rejoice in his gain of eternal life with our Lord and Savior Jesus Christ. My father *is* alive and is forever set free from the power of sin and death. We will walk together again, only next time it will be on streets of gold! Walter Martin's grave marker reads, "I rest my case," and indeed he had, after giving a lifelong defense of the gospel on the world's stage. His favorite hymn was "Amazing Grace." I can still recall seeing him joyfully sing it with his class at Melodyland. His life verse was Jude 3: "Contend earnestly for the faith once for all delivered to the Saints."

Shortly after his death, I wrote a song to honor my father's life. It describes the kind of warrior he was for the gospel of Jesus Christ:

---

[2] Author Unknown, "Safely Home." There have been varying versions of this poem, and Danny quoted a version slightly different from the one at Bible.org, https://bible.org/illustration/safely-home.

[3] Cindee Martin Morgan, "Walter Martin Honored by Son-in-Law Rick Morgan at His Memorial Service June 29, 1989," YouTube video, 7:20, published January 18, 2009, https://www.youtube.com/watch?v=ErkpMC0iDf4.

[4] Cindee Martin Morgan, "Walter Martin Honored by Brother-in-Law/CRI Board Member Everett Jacobson," YouTube video, 4:24, published February 1, 2009, https://www.youtube.com/watch?v=OxstMHvuTTU.

The Bible Answer Man
Walter Martin and Hank Hanegraaff

"Soldier of the Cross"

Proclaiming the gospel was your call;
Determined to give Him your all.
The way was not always clear,
Some pathways were filled with fear.
But He saw you through, as He promised to.

You were a soldier of the cross, a life well spent.
You were a soldier of the cross, you knew what victory meant.
With the armor of God and the shield of faith;
You marched on with the Victor,
And won the race!

Our fellow warrior wounded in the fight;
Our brother in Jesus we lost in the night.
What joy you must have known,
To kneel at His throne!
A warrior in Jesus
Our brother, in Jesus,
Well done!

All those who've gone before us;
All the soldiers that marched in the battle of truth and His cause.
We will one day meet, as we kneel at His feet.
For the battle is done!
One day with God's Son,
All the soldiers of His army —
All the soldiers of the cross;
Will stand in His kingdom with joy and in freedom,
And hear Him say, well done!
The race is run — the battle's done — well done!

Heaven shall be a place of perfect rest and peace. Those who dwell there have no more conflict with the world, the flesh, and the devil; their warfare is accomplished, and their fight is fought; at length they may lay aside the armor of God, at last they may say to the sword of the Spirit, Rest and be still.

They watch no longer, for they have no spiritual enemies to fear...Their sin and temptation are forever shut out; the gates are better barred than those of Eden, and the Devil shall enter in no more.

—J. C. Ryle

The Bible Answer Man
Walter Martin and Hank Hanegraaff

What was it like in the aftermath of my father's homegoing? It helped that Rick, our children, and me were living with Jill and Kevin at the start of our new Minnesota life. It was evident the Lord had intended for us to comfort one another in a way we could not have done from a distance.

As we grieved, I found myself looking around at strangers on occasion and thinking, "Why are *you* still here, and my father is gone?!" I asked God what he was thinking, taking my dad at the age of sixty. Once in a blue moon, I'd see someone from the side, or from behind, who looked like my dad — wishing it were him. I discovered I didn't know who I was without him. It occurred to me that much of my identity was wrapped up in being Walter Martin's daughter. For twenty-eight years, I had seen myself through that lens. I was thrilled to be wife and mother of three, but I had first been his daughter — his child. I enjoyed when people shared with me how much the *Bible Answer Man* was ministering to their lives.

I loved hearing my father's stories, and spending time with him. Now he was gone, and I had to speak of him, along with everyone else, in the past tense. In my mind's eye, the reality of heaven grew by leaps and bounds, which is why Joni's song especially blessed me during this season of our lives. Day by day, the Lord began to paint the broken pieces of my life with visions of golden streets, angels, blue skies, my father, and other loved ones already in heaven. More than ever before, I could imagine Jesus's outstretched arms waiting there to greet me, and yes, we would dance. The following dance, I pray, will be with my earthly father as I begin my waltz of eternal life with Jesus Christ, my Lord, in the home He's prepared for me. The last gift I gave my dad was the CD *Somewhere in Time*, which he loved. From time to time, I still listen to it. It is yet another reminder that my father *is* alive. He *exists* somewhere in the supernatural time zone of eternity.

Shortly after my father relocated to his heavenly dwelling, I went to a chiropractor because my neck was locked in one position. He took an X-ray and gave me an adjustment which immediately fixed the problem. I had no idea I was pregnant at the time — nor what an X-ray could mean for an unborn child. Within a week of learning about my pregnancy, I began having complications. We called an obstetrician, who told me to stay in bed and that I didn't need an office visit. Jill took care of me while Rick was at work. It helped we were all still living together. I needed my sister. It took three days for me to miscarry. Rick finally had to take me to the emergency room. A nurse told us that the X-ray, more than likely, had caused me to miscarry. As many parents know, losing a child causes an emptiness that runs deep. What eventually helped us the most was imagining my father's joy as he embraced his newest grandbaby, whom Rick and I named Joshua. We believed they were together and that one day we would be reunited. I knew the Lord and Grandad Martin would watch over our little one for me.

9

FOR THE SAKE OF TRUTH

"Controversy for the sake of controversy is sin. Controversy for the sake of the truth is a divine command." —Walter Martin

For six years following my father's death, my stepmom Darlene served on the board of CRI along with Hank Hanegraaff, Everett Jacobson (my father's former brother-in-law), and other board members. Although no longer related to my dad by marriage, my Uncle Everett had remained a faithful friend to him. They considered themselves brothers. My uncle had never had a brother before knowing my father and was never going to give him up.

About four years after Darlene's departure from the board, a major storm hit CRI's horizon; a slow-acting poison was injected into the bloodstream of its reputation that required an antidote. The ministry Walter Martin had gone to such great lengths to protect was in danger. The way the Lord provided the cure — using an ex-CRI employee-turned-atheist to unwittingly deliver the antidote — was nothing short of a miracle. The antidote itself would allow Walter Martin to protect CRI from the grave. I am certain my father never imagined what would happen to this ministry *ten years* after the Lord called him home.

The year was now 1999, and Hank Hanegraaff had been president for a decade. Accusations emerged in a secular newspaper that Hank had *stolen* his leadership position at CRI. Stories on the internet erupted that he was merely hired by Walter Martin for his fundraising and management abilities. A lie was promoted that they were never even friends. The internet that Walter Martin utilized to make CRI a global blessing was now being used in an effort to destroy everything he'd built. After ten years at the helm, Hank was accused of having obtained his position in a nefarious way. This painful accusation was a threatening blow to this ministry. While those in leadership within the walls of CRI knew my father had chosen Hank, others were publicly demanding proof. Some insisted Walter Martin would never hire anyone to lead CRI who had not yet completed his degree.

Everett Jacobson was on CRI's board and had been there *for more than forty years serving with both Walter Martin and Hank Hanegraaff*. He assured me my father had chosen Hank and was astonished this was ever an issue. Everett Jacobson explained that he had taken the minutes himself at board meetings countless times, for many years, and *during my father's last days*. These minutes described Hank's unique place at the ministry the Lord had called him to. Everett Jacobson was a man rich with integrity. He strongly respected Hank and what he was doing at CRI for the Kingdom of God.

At my father's memorial service, John Ankerberg told everyone of his first-hand knowledge of Walter Martin choosing Hank to lead CRI into the future. He mentioned how he'd prayed with Hank, in October of 1988, about his decision whether to accept the vice president position. CRI's editor-in-chief, Elliot Miller, was a first-hand witness as well. He was one of its first employees when my father moved CRI to California, back in the 1970s. Elliot was with CRI until the Lord called him home early last year. He was a true soldier of the Cross. In spite of substantial first-hand testimony, CRI found itself hit with a wave of suspicion. Rick and I were disheartened that the ministry my father fought so hard to protect was now forced to defend itself in the court of public opinion.

At the time of my father's death, several men came forward, each claiming that Walter Martin had been grooming them to take his place. The truth, however, is that Walter Martin saw ministry gifts *in Hank* that greatly impressed him; he was convinced he was the *only one* at the time who had the ability to lead CRI. The bottom line is that Walter Martin chose Hank to take his place because he had confidence in his God-given gifts. My father had a history of hiring researchers on occasion who did not have *any* earned degree. My father's friend, Walter Bjorck — a CRI researcher—*never* earned one, and he filled in for Walter Martin on the *Bible Answer Man* program countless times back in the 1960s. This is consistent with what Elliot Miller once told me. He explained that while my father believed an education is important, and often said so, he was wise enough to hire people to work for him *if* their ministry gifts were exceptional and he recognized the Lord's calling on their life to serve at CRI. This ought to help dispel the notion that Walter Martin was an intellectual or theological snob; this was not the case. His heart was open to whatever *the will of God* might be for CRI. He knew that CRI is a ministry God set in motion.

CRI veteran board member Everett Jacobson — my uncle and dear friend — died in 2007. He used to call me every month or two, after losing my dad, to inquire how our family was doing and how he could pray for us. A few years later, it became evident God was leading Rick and me to become a part of this ministry. Hank hired Rick to be CRI's webmaster and social media director. I went online to support CRI and to promote my father's legacy in as many ways as possible. This was when the Lord gave me the antidote — the evidence — CRI needed to extract the poison that was morphing into a major threat to a ministry fiercely fighting for the souls of men.

At the time of his death, I was personally unaware of whom my father chose to lead CRI, but I became convinced by the first-hand testimony of many witnesses. Knowing both my father and Hank personally, I became convinced Walter Martin saw some of himself in Hank. Hank is well taught, articulate, has extraordinary memory retention, a love for the lost, and was eager to take on the enormous responsibility of CRI. The added bonus was that Hank was also a good office manager. That was a gift my dad did not believe he, himself, possessed.

With a heavy heart, I told the Lord I wished I could hear my father's voice speaking about his leadership plans; I wanted to help this ministry he loved so much. I obviously knew that God wouldn't raise my father from the dead to speak with me about this. I was simply pouring out my frustration before His throne. Only weeks prior to me laying this burden down before the Lord, I had joined YouTube. Within weeks following my talk with God about wanting to hear my father's voice, I was contacted by someone *by way of YouTube*. He was a disgruntled ex-CRI employee-turned-atheist, whom I had never met, asking me if I would like to have hundreds of audiotapes he had taken from CRI. (I later learned he may have stolen these tapes and had been selling them on the internet for personal profit.) He briefly explained he no longer believed in God, but that he loved Walter Martin. He said he wanted me to have the tapes; I accepted, not having a clue how valuable they would prove to be. I received two boxes that were each a few feet tall. As I looked through them, I noticed that a handful of tapes were marked to indicate Walter Martin speaking about his leadership plans for CRI. I was shocked by this swift and unique answer to my prayer. As I listened to them, the Lord enabled me, in a real sense, to enter an audio time tunnel and hear my dad's own words setting the record straight now and forever. It was a hug from heaven — a supernatural blast from the past — to be given this unique opportunity to hear CRI's founder discuss an issue that had become a serious threat to this ministry. It also explained why CRI didn't have possession of the audio evidence with which to defend itself.

After I'd received the tapes, the atheist wrote to let me know he would be posting videos of Hank in an effort to destroy his reputation; sadly, he was under the impression this would please us. He mistakenly thought we opposed Hank's leadership at CRI. When he discovered that Rick and I supported CRI, he was furious he had sent us anything. To his horror, he had unwittingly shipped me a time capsule that came from both an earthly and heavenly zip code. Little did he know that it was *God's will* that he would be bowing to, whether he wanted to or not. God chose to use a professed enemy of the cross for His own purposes, just as He did in the days of Moses, and does to this day. It is nothing short of miraculous that God allowed CRI's own founder to defend the ministry God raised up through him, *after he had been home with the Lord for twenty years!* Only God can do such a thing.

Many don't realize that, on occasion, Hank would speak to Walter Martin's Bible class and was representing CRI in Brazil during the time my father was carving out a place for him at CRI.

The following Walter Martin quotes are a major portion of the antidote the Lord provided by way of the Bible class tapes. After two years of planning and praying, Walter Martin excitedly announced to his Bible class, "I've been praying for one man, for two years, that God would put it on his heart.... And God *did* put it on his heart.... He can run the entire operation and is *very, very* good in the world of the cults and is an excellent and very successful man in his own right..... I ask you to pray for this person who would be number two person in our structure at CRI, and he's a godly man. The Lord has used him in a mighty way down south and in other parts of the country, and we've asked him to join us. He said he is willing to. So, now we're in the praying stages and asking God to work out all the details of it. He'll probably be a vice president or an executive director at CRI, and I *badly* need someone like that.... We want the best we can get, and this gentleman we believe is the best on the horizon, so please be in prayer about that."[1]

On another occasion, he described Hank to his class as "someone with the credentials and the ability. Somebody that could teach, somebody that could preach. Somebody who had the capacity to manage and has been very successful in his own operation for some time. This is somebody in whom I have implicit confidence.... I do not believe the myth of invulnerability or of immortality. I've seen too many Christian leaders think that they were never going to die and wait until the last minute before they got anybody to help them, and then they had chaos. I have not made that mistake."[2]

Two months prior to his death, Walter Martin introduced Hank Hanegraaff to his Bible class as the new *executive vice president* of CRI. It was

---

[1] From a recording of Walter Martin's Bible Study class, October 23, 1988. Copyright Christian Research Institute.
[2] From a recording of Walter Martin's Bible Study class, December 4, 1988. Copyright Christian Research Institute.

critical to my father that the ministry God had entrusted him with live beyond its founder. He took this responsibility seriously and faithfully took measures to protect CRI. Two months prior to his death, he joyfully announced to his Sunday school class, "We got a real special treat this morning; I'm just so happy about it. Hank Hanegraaff has just come back from Brazil, where he went to survey our ministry down there, and he has an exciting report for us. So, I'm going to answer the questions, and then I'm going to let Hank talk with you about the evangelism in Brazil.... Will you welcome back from the wilds of Brazil the executive vice president of Christian Research Institute, and my friend, Hank Hanegraaff."[3]

Walter Martin made his choice. Jesus's disciples did not have degrees hanging on their walls; they were not chosen because they were well taught, like the Pharisees. While formal theological training *is* valuable, so are lives without it dedicated to serving the Lord. Jesus chose men according to *the will of God*. Walter Martin believed it was the will of God to hire Hank to be his executive vice president. Walter Martin saw *value* in Hank Hanegraaff; he *knew* Hank. Choosing him was not a last-minute decision. My father prayed for one man for two years. He *vetted* Hank, mentored him for a leadership position, and set into motion his plan for CRI.

I have heard from countless people who are happy to hear what Walter Martin's plans were for CRI. We have received emails from some who were in his Bible class at that time, who mentioned they remember praying for Hank regarding his executive vice president position and becoming Walter Martin's successor. Those who continue to accuse Hank of the crime of stealing CRI are most likely motivated by misunderstanding, professional jealousy, or — in some cases — theological bias. The bottom line is this: Walter Martin's words matter, because truth matters. His words should be respected, not ignored or redefined. It *is* unusual that the children of Walter Martin did not realize he'd chosen Hank as his successor back in 1989. Knowing my father, I believe he did not want to upset us by mentioning he was looking for a man *to replace him in the event of his death*. My siblings and I had no idea, at the time, how ill he was. I believe our dad decided to trust the Lord to comfort us, when the time came for him to leave us.

On a side note, I will answer a frequently asked question involving CRI's Walter Martin resources, owned by the ministry. Why is CRI not airing its audio recordings of Walter Martin from time to time on the *Bible Answer Man* program? When my older sister and her husband began their own ministry

---

[3] WalterMartinJude3, "Walter Martin Introduces Hank Hanegraaff As Executive Vice President of CRI 04-09-89," YouTube video, 2:10, published August 1, 2011, https://www.youtube.com/watch?v=g_FyV6PElFI.

about twenty years ago, they asked CRI if their ministry could be an outlet for airing these audio recordings. Out of deference to my stepmother, Darlene, Hank allowed the Martin family use of the material. Many YouTube users (and others) have posted, *without permission*, CRI Walter Martin audio recordings throughout the years; Hank graciously allows it all *for the sake of the gospel*. He has never threatened copyright infringement claims, as some ministries do. Will CRI one day air their Walter Martin resources again themselves? It is my prayer they will. It would be wonderful for my father to be heard through as many sources as possible, especially the ministry he founded.

After Rick and I received the Walter Martin audiotapes — from the ex-CRI employee — ten years ago, we shared my father's words with some of our extended family. We were thankful to the Lord for the miracle that allowed CRI's founder to personally set the record straight via YouTube and other venues. Our joy, however, would be temporary. We soon witnessed our clips of Walter Martin (speaking of his plans for CRI) hit with copyright infringement claims by some who opposed Hank's role at CRI. Walter Martin himself, in a real sense, was being censored. A public notice went up in place where the clips had been on our channels. The world was informed that Rick and I were being accused of a federal crime. Our YouTube channels were put at risk. Our Christian testimony was challenged because many visitors trying to view the videos would not know I am Walter Martin's daughter. These false accusations against us were made in an effort to prevent us from posting *my father's own words* spoken to his Bible class, shortly before his death, about his plans for CRI. It was intense spiritual warfare; poisonous arrows hit us after we had excitedly shared what God had done for this ministry. This was not the response we had prayed for, and it short-circuited us emotionally. The oppression on our lives was intense. YouTube eventually reversed the copyright infringement claims, and Walter Martin was once again heard on our YouTube channels.

In the aftermath of that, more arrows — via a lawsuit — shot through our door after we refused to remove what YouTube had reinstated. I will never forget the day we were served. I was babysitting my first grandson when the doorbell rang, in the summer of 2010. I opened the door with him in my arms. The young man hesitated, shifted his feet a bit, and said something like, "I apologize I have to serve you. I read some of this...." He looked so sad, I thought he might try to hug me.

I immediately noticed CRI was being sued along with us. Rick and I grappled with what seemed a bad dream from which we couldn't wake. We prayed about how to best respond. Although a fierce soldier of the cross, my husband was in the process of grieving the recent death of his father, and he ended up being hospitalized for a heart attack.

The Bible Answer Man
Walter Martin and Hank Hanegraaff

As this surreal chapter of our lives unfolded, I must confess, I was undone. It felt like we were aging rapidly. I pleaded with God to let this cup pass from us. We knew, however, that God wanted *us* to share my father's words — and the miracle of the tapes — to support CRI, but it was the greatest challenge we'd ever known. Whenever our phone rang, I feared it was our attorney with updates. I struggled with the prospect of losing everything due to the expense the lawsuit was inflicting. Our youngest daughter, Katie — the only one still living at home with us — feared she might soon be homeless. Rick and I earnestly prayed the Lord would never allow us to lose the ability to help our children and grandchildren.

In an effort to cover our mounting costs, we explored our insurance policies to see if we had any applicable coverage. We were promptly served by one of our own insurance providers at the time, who told us that unless we signed a paper stating they were not responsible to cover us — for any of our current lawsuit costs — *they* would file a lawsuit against us also! Yes, you read that correctly. They threatened us for merely *inquiring* if we had a certain type of coverage. In order to stop this second lawsuit, we had to agree not to tell anyone publicly who we were covered by during that time or publicly connect them to the wrong they were doing against us. This was, without question, a crafty form of spiritual warfare. Needless to say, we agreed to their terms. Rick and I are able to laugh now about the bizarre fact we were served *twice* during this intense spiritual battle, but we were *not* laughing then. I'd like to be able to say I was a rock during at least part of this drama-laced season, but the opposite is true. Although I was determined not to allow my father to be silenced, Rick was *my* rock as we repeatedly implored the Rock of Ages to deliver us from evil. Our pastor at the time, Stephen Lonetti, our church, and godly friends steadfastly stood by us through it all, which brought a great deal of comfort.

This lawsuit is a part of CRI's history. Effective ministries are often ensnared in controversy when seeking to reach a lost world for Jesus Christ.

I recognize there is an elephant in the room of this story. Who attacked our Walter Martin clips on our YouTube channels? Ironically, it was the *same sister and brother-in-law* who received access to CRI's material two decades ago. Those who are aware of the ongoing public attacks on CRI already know their names because *they* have openly identified themselves. Sadly, they have insisted Hank Hanegraaff was not chosen by Walter Martin to lead CRI and have repeatedly inferred he stole his position. The clips contradict their position.

Rick and I were horrified to be falsely and publicly accused of copyright infringement especially given the fact it is a crime that can carry serious consequences. Worse yet, for the first time in my adult life, I was being ordered not to share my own father's words. To the best of our knowledge, no one else posting Walter Martin audio clips on YouTube was targeted.

Who sued Rick and me? We, along with CRI, were sued by a different family member who relayed that she had been urged to file a lawsuit by the sister and brother-in-law whose ministry was graciously permitted the use of CRI's Walter Martin material for the past twenty years. It grieved our hearts to learn of my sister's informal participation in the lawsuit, behind the scenes.

God says His children will be held accountable if we do nothing in the face of evil. Rick and I can't be silent. Hank is not guilty of something CRI's own founder says he has not done. God positioned and equipped us to stand in the truth and to right the wrong being done against a ministry that God began while I was still in my mother's womb. Hank's children and grandchildren should have his legacy as CRI's second president left intact, without the historical shadows of false accusations. Paul, in 2 Timothy 4:14, mentions that Alexander the Coppersmith did him great harm. On occasion, it is necessary to respond to evil publicly. Due to the negative impact this story has had on a ministry, it must be told.

To more fully understand what led to this conflict, I will give some of the back story. The family member who sued us wholeheartedly agreed that Walter Martin *had* chosen Hank after listening to the tapes the atheist had sent to Rick and me. She expressed deep concern that the information would upset my oldest sister. We spent three days visiting and discussing my father's words. We had great fellowship. We also attended a church service together at her church. Ironically, the pastor opened his sermon with Walter Martin's life verse, Jude 3, and asked his congregation if they'd ever been the victim of a rumor. We were at peace with this loved one when we left her home, and felt united in the truth, but that would be short lived. Rick and I were quickly warned that if we didn't remove the audio clips from YouTube, there would be serious consequences.

To add additional perspective, it must be emphasized that my sister's ongoing accusation that Hank stole CRI began when he had already been president for *ten* years. She has never worked for CRI, does not know Hank Hanegraaff personally, did not know Elliot Miller, nor did she have a relationship with our uncle Everett after her childhood. I love my sister dearly; I believe she *thinks* that what she is doing is right, but she is *desperately* wrong. God warns us not to bear false witness against our neighbor.

In my opinion, some of my family members were deceived by disgruntled ex-CRI employees who had managed to make inroads with them. I also believe that secondary theological differences helped to cloud perspectives. When we were sued, another disgruntled ex-CRI employee contacted me to scold Rick and I for publicly standing by CRI. He was not offended that we, or this ministry, was being sued. We were saddened by this but knew this man was someone my father wanted fired for his yellow journalism tactics, years back, and were not surprised by this misguided affront.

In the heat of this spiritual battle, I had an important conversation with our former pastor, Bill Phillips. I was tempted to run from the battlefield. I was exhausted on every level, and my health was suffering. The battle was fierce, and I was weary. I will never forget Pastor Bill's words. He said something like, "Cindee, if not you, then *who*? Who besides you and Rick can do this? God has called you to stand. He brought the truth to your door by way of an atheist you had never met. You must stand firm! He is with you." I immediately sensed an urging from the Lord to not give up. Hearing our pastor's words reminded me that I am not a part-time soldier of the cross; I am in the battle until the Lord calls me home. With the miracle God gave, in hand, I tried to rest in the promise that "I can do all things through Christ who strengthens me" (Philippians 4:13). Pastor Bill taught us to "obey the Lord *even when you don't feel like it*. If you wait until you do, you *won't* obey. *Obey Him*, and the feelings will follow." I learned there is enormous blessing that comes when we do our Father's will, and especially so when the cost is high. We counted it, and we paid the price. We suffered and are still suffering. Our burden, however, does not hold a candle to those who have lost *their very lives* for Christ, nor does our struggle come anywhere near the price Jesus paid for His children on the cross of Calvary.

Many people put an ungodly emphasis on family loyalty, but God tells us that we, His children, *must be loyal to Him*. CRI does not belong to a family; it belongs to the Lord. We believe the historical evidence — underscored by Walter Martin's own statements — is in perfect harmony with the firsthand testimonies. My father was a faithful soldier of the Cross, and because of that, he also has my loyalty.

As this trial ended, it became evident to us that God had parted the sea and we had walked to the other side stronger in the Lord than we'd ever been before. We praise God that the lawsuit was dismissed many years ago and thankful that we also had opportunity to witness to our Jewish attorney. We seek to live each day walking in this truth — the Lord has our backs, and His track record is perfect. We thank God for sustaining and protecting us.

By the grace of God, we live at peace with most of our extended family members, including the loved one who sued us. We have often sought reconciliation with my sister and brother-in-law. Please pray they will seek godly counsel with us some day, that relationships will be healed, and that God will be glorified by our reconciliation. We pray God will to do above and beyond anything we could think or ask, believing He is able.

10

A THEOLOGICAL BLAST FROM THE PAST: THE LOCAL CHURCH AND CRI

In many ways, the stand Walter Martin took on The Seventh Day Adventists back in the '60s reminds me of the stand CRI took on the Local Church Movement of Watchman Nee and Witness Lee in 2009 under the leadership of Hank Hanegraaff. CRI privately and publicly withstood the same type of criticisms Walter Martin and Donald Barnhouse endured by determining that the Local Church, like Seventh Day Adventism, contained the core doctrines of Christianity. Hank agreed with the findings of Gretchen Passantino — *who had spearheaded the research of the Local Church, for Walter Martin, decades earlier* — and Elliot Miller, *who also had played a major role in the research provided to Walter Martin.* Their findings this time around, however, were vastly different than what they and others presented to CRI's first president. Based on two of its top researchers' earliest assessment, CRI expressed serious concerns in its 1980 book *The New Cults,* stating in its Appendix:

> It should be mentioned at the outset that the Local Church and its leader, Witness Lee, are different from the other groups we are dealing with in this book in that by and large the Local Church is composed of Christians who have been confused about major areas of doctrine and Christian practice. We must be sure to distinguish between the *doctrines and practices* of this group, which are not in harmony with the Bible, and the *members* of the Local Church, who are confused Christians. Technically speaking, the Local Church of Witness Lee cannot be called a non-Christian cult, but it has strong

elements of cultism is some of its theology and practices.[1]

It was concluded, however, that the Local Church was not "technically" a cult. It is important to emphasize that Walter Martin was not the author of *The New Cults*. It was written by the CRI research staff with Gretchen featured as its most prominent contributor. Walter Martin was the general editor, with Gretchen Passantino's name featured under his, in smaller print, followed by the names of seven other CRI researchers — which included Elliot Miller — and a second mention of Gretchen's name. It is explicitly stated that "Gretchen Passantino contributed significantly to the research of this book, and also contributed the writing of the manuscript."[2] It is imperative to note that my father relied heavily on Gretchen for the conclusions drawn about the Local Church in the Appendix of *The New Cults* as well as the rest of the information presented in the book. It should be noted also that there is *not* an actual chapter devoted to the Local Church in this work.

More than twenty years later, after devoting six years to a deeper theological investigation, Gretchen and Elliot convinced CRI's current president *they* had been wrong and had made major errors regarding their first assessment. They came to believe they mistakenly had misled Walter Martin. CRI's most current assessment, by Gretchen and Elliot, can be found in an entire edition of a CRI JOURNAL, entitled *We Were Wrong*.[3]

It is significant to note that both CRI presidents historically concurred with Gretchen Passantino's findings, each valuing her lion's share of the research done on the Local Church. I remember how much my father respected and esteemed Gretchen's contributions to CRI and how much he valued Elliot Miller; he often mentioned this to me. This is the reason Rick and I give their research a great deal of credit. While Walter Martin greatly valued his entire staff, no other researchers were ever mentioned to me as many times as were Gretchen and Elliot. Walter Martin was both professionally and personally involved with them. They were close friends with CRI's past and present presidents. Walter Martin and Hank Hanegraaff both loved these two exceptional theological minds and lives committed to serving our Lord Jesus Christ. Rick and I are blessed to have known these faithful soldiers of the cross. Both Gretchen and Elliot were tremendous

---

[1] Walter Martin, ed., *The New Cults*, with Gretchen Passantino and the CRI Research Staff (Ventura, CA: GL Regal Books, 1980).
[2] Martin, *The New Cults*, 410.
[3] *Christian Research Journal* vol. 32, 6 (2009), available to download in several languages at https://www.equip.org/Christian-research-journal/we-were-wrong-2/.

assets to CRI in Walter Martin's day and during the time Hank has been there.

Hank devoted an entire CRI JOURNAL issue to the Local Church because he became convinced that they indeed believe the essential doctrines of Christianity. This new research was never intended to be a criticism of Walter Martin; it was intended to be a public acknowledgment that the ministry of CRI — past and present — had come full circle and now has a different theological opinion. Whether or not you agree with Gretchen Passantino and Elliot Miller, then-editor-in-chief of CRI's JOURNAL, they are two of the *same prominent researchers* Walter Martin trusted to biblically vet the Local Church when he was at the helm of CRI. He had confidence in them; he relied on their research. *That is compelling.* Would he have agreed with their lengthier in-depth research and final conclusions? Only the Lord knows for certain, but I believe there's a strong possibility he would have. Gretchen and Elliot wisely determined that semantics were to blame for much of the confusion surrounding this controversial debate.

Members of the Local Church have suffered severe persecution in China because of the research CRI had done decades earlier. Some endured prison because they had come extremely close to being labeled a "cult." Gretchen and Elliot, yet again, did tedious and more extensive research that led them to a far different conclusion. They *searched things out* and honored their conscience before God by seeking to set the record straight. They humbled themselves, grieved over their initial assessment of the Local Church, and sought their forgiveness — Gretchen did this in person, on her knees. I urge those wanting a deeper theological understanding of the Local Church to prayerfully consider Gretchen and Elliot's most current assessment of their doctrine, for the sake of the gospel.

Hank Hanegraaff was deeply affected by his visits to persecuted Christians in China. I asked him about this in an email exchange. Hank responded:

> Those encounters not only changed me but forever altered our ministry. These interactions were occasioned as a result of our intensive research into the teachings and practices of the Local Church movement of Watchman Nee and Witness Lee.
>
> In the West, theology, like politics, has become a veritable blood sport. In the East, things are somewhat different. More than a conceptual framework of faith, theology means something closer to the literal meaning of the word ("Theos" meaning *God* and "logos" connoting *knowledge*). Thus, far from signifying arguments about God, theology signified intimacy and communion with God. The creature encountering the Creator. The theoretical (though important) overshadowed by a living intimacy with the One who knit

us together in our mother's wombs.

This is precisely what I experienced during our primary research on the Local Church movement. The very people we were critiquing exemplified something beyond truth. They personified life. They proved to be humble Christians, so united with Christ that they naturally did the works of Christ. It was not that they considered truth to be unnecessary; they simply recognized it to be insufficient.

One morning as I was flying back from East to West, I found myself staring into the clouds, pondering my own Christian experience. I had spent the better part of my career defining truth, debating truth, defending truth. I knew what I believed and why I believed it. Yet it had become clear to me that the Christians I had encountered in the underground church of China were experiencing something beyond truth. They were experiencing life that is life to the full.

As I stared into the vast expanse of the heavens from the vantage of my window seat, the great medieval theologian Thomas Aquinas flashed through my mind. Thomas had committed the whole of his mortal existence to the examination and explication of truth — his *Summa Theologica* roundly regarded as one of the greatest intellectual accomplishments in all of Western civilization. His life's work was to codify all of truth into one coherent whole — truth from the findings of anthropology, science, ethics, psychology, political theory, and theology all under God.

But on the morning of December 6, 1273, Thomas had a eucharistic encounter with the real presence of God that radically rearranged his priorities. On that morning he had an experience that so viscerally impacted his being that the *Summa* was left unfinished. While celebrating Holy Communion in the Chapel, he caught a glimpse of eternity. He was given a revelation from God that let him know that all his efforts to describe God fell so far short that he decided to never write again. When his secretary and friend, Reginald, tried to encourage him to do more writing, he said, "Reginald, I can do no more. The end of my labors has come. Such things have been revealed to me that all I have written seems as so much straw."

My experience was not as immediate. Nor as dramatic. At least not at first. Yet standing for truth on behalf of the Local Churches has become my portal into life. The lifeblood of another has been ingrafted within me and even now I am experiencing union with God. Watchman Nee was right to say that salvation is far more than justification. That it is nothing short of deification.[4] "To bring God into man, making God one with man as a God-man." Nee's language might have been unnerving to detractors, but it was hardly novel. Orthodox theologian Vladimir Lossky, born the same year as Nee (1903), said much the same thing. "After the Fall, human history is a long shipwreck awaiting rescue: but the port of salvation is not the goal; it is the possibility for the shipwrecked to resume his journey whose sole goal is union with God."[5]

The concept of deification, though rarely discussed in Protestant theology, is a Christian doctrine taught in the church, from the earliest church fathers, through the Reformers. This doctrine teaches that man may become *like* God, while never implying that man can *become* God.

Hank Hanegraaff's forthcoming book *Truth Matters; Life Matters More* sets forth his story. Without question, most American Christians have no idea what it's like to endure severe persecution — the kind our brothers and sisters around the world endure to this day. Hank's experiences and insights are a gift to the body of Christ.

---

[4] Gregg R. Allison, *Baker Compact Dictionary of Theological Terms* (Grand Rapids: Baker Books, 2016).
[5] This was a personal email to the author from Hank Hanegraaff.

11

WALTER MARTIN'S VIEWS

Elliot Miller wrote a book shortly before the Lord called him home — *The Odd Faith Out: The Uniqueness of Biblical Spiritual Experiences*. After his death, his dear wife, Corinne, shared with me that his book "is about the differences between spiritual faiths and that which Christians believe. Christianity is the odd faith out." While Elliot didn't live to see his newest work published, there is no doubt in my mind it will be a blessing to the body of Christ. I enjoy imagining this dear brother in heaven chatting with my father about what went on, for God's glory, at and through CRI since God called Walter Martin home in 1989. They have forever to catch up as they rejoice for all eternity in the house of the Lord.

Rick and I were disappointed to learn about a book (*The Kingdom of the Occult*) written in Walter Martin's name almost *twenty years* after his death. His name takes up almost half of its front cover with the words, "From the Author of *The Kingdom of the Cults*" printed above it. Two additional names are cited, in much smaller print, under Walter Martin's name — his eldest daughter being one of them. Sadly, my sister is at the center of yet another controversy that hit us head-on. The way *The Kingdom of the Occult* is written makes Walter Martin appear to directly assert that he condemned certain end-times interpretations held by many Evangelical Christians as aberrant theology and evidence of satanic influence in the church, but that is the direct opposite of what my father taught. This is false and unintentionally sows division in the body of Christ.

A few brief quotes from *The Kingdom of the Occult*:

Signs of the occult revolution are everywhere today — even within the Church....

- Key biblical doctrines are reinterpreted. The book of Revelation, for example, might be presented as "fulfilled" and Israel's biblical significance diminished or dismissed.

- The modern Church becomes the new "Israel." In this view, also known as replacement theology, God has abandoned Israel for his adopted children, a twisting of biblical theology that the apostle Paul refuted.[1]

First, I should emphasize that this is not what those who oppose dispensationalism believe. In the love of Christ, I must point out that replacement theology *is a pejorative term* that is used by some to attempt to silence the opponents of dispensational theology and to discourage independent study of the opposing views. It refers to a theological view poorly understood by many dispensationalists. The true doctrine is frequently misrepresented but is held by vast numbers in the church. I will briefly cite a partial quote of Walter Martin's (about one year prior to his death) in response to *The Kingdom of the Occult's* statements, as I've already well documented my father's beliefs regarding this doctrine.

Walter Martin stated in 1987, "Do not ever make the mistake of believing that National Israel today, in Palestine or Israel, is the Israel of God, because they are not; they cannot be until they repent of their sin and until they confess that Jesus Christ is God and Savior — that He is truly the Messiah."[2]

The Kingdom of the Occult would have caused Walter Martin to have righteous indignation because it does not represent him accurately. The way the text is written, it is *impossible* for the reader to discern which of the authors is speaking. Worse yet, Walter Martin would not support a book written in his name and done without his knowledge. (I don't believe many would.) Elliot Miller, CRI's then-editor-in-chief, informed me of this. Knowing my father, it does not surprise me that is the case. To add insult to injury, the book *contradicts* his own beliefs and has the potential of harming Walter Martin's tireless efforts to warn future generations (should the Lord tarry) not to divide over what he considered a secondary issue. My father promoted unity.

---

[1] Walter Martin, Jill Martin Rische, and Kurt Van Gordon, *The Kingdom of the Occult* (Nashville: Thomas Nelson, 2008).
[2] From a recording of Walter Martin's Bible Study class, May 3, 1987. Copyright Christian Research Institute.

The Bible Answer Man
Walter Martin and Hank Hanegraaff

Rick became aware of the error in this book in a Christian chat room. He became a witness to a serious discussion underway between a Walter Martin fan and his father-in-law's eldest daughter. The fan was extremely upset that Walter Martin's views were being distorted in a book with his name on it. Rick decided to join the conversation anonymously in a sincere effort to help them both. I know Rick's heart. He thought that by helping my sister set the record straight, she would then be able to correct an error in the next edition of this book. Given the fact that my sister had left our lives, Rick believed the Lord was leading him to join this conversation, as he would not have been allowed to participate as himself — he felt desperate times call for desperate measures.

Rick was kind and sought to turn the situation around in a constructive way by quoting Walter Martin's own words in several of his posts. Instead of responding positively to the information Rick brought to the table, his sister-in-law held her ground. Completely exasperated, we decided to approach another family member about this issue. She shared our concern, appeared to understand Rick's decision to speak about this in a chat room, agreed to intervene in the hope of correcting the situation, and persuaded my sister to do as we asked — to meet with us and discuss her book. We were extremely disappointed the meeting did not bring the resolution we had prayed for. We shared the chat room exchanges with our pastor at the time, Stephen Lonetti. Pastor Steve is a dispensationalist but recognizes that Walter Martin's eschatological beliefs *are* distorted in *The Kingdom of the Occult* book. He assured us Rick's actions were appropriate and that his responses, in the chat room, were godly.

Rick and I came away from this difficult confrontation with a peace that we dealt with this issue as the Lord led. We did email one (non-family) author of this book in the hope he could help us correct their book, but it was futile; *he insisted my father was a dispensationalist* and sought to convince us we were mistaken.

It is troubling to recall that during this season of time, Walter Martin's sermon "The Tribulation and the Church" (his self-described end-times beliefs) was removed temporarily from our Walter Martin Jude 3 YouTube channel because of false copyright infringement claims made by my sister and brother-in-law. We thank the Lord the truth regarding what my father believed, up until his death, remains available. Without question, he makes his views *crystal clear* in this message (and in many others).

Walter Martin's beliefs, while not currently as popular in our day as dispensationalism, are nonetheless held by many in the Evangelical community and are deeply rooted in orthodox theology. Charles Spurgeon, R. C. Sproul, John Piper, Tim Keller, Ken Gentry, and many other godly teachers are *not* dispensationalists.

Why discuss this now? A new generation is being taught that Walter Martin believed things he often spoke out against. In addition, nothing has been corrected. I spent a year and a half researching this book. There is no evidence my father embraced dispensationalism, after he came to reject its claims time and time again. I recall him, up until when the Lord called him home, gently trying to discourage Christians from embracing this theology.

Walter Martin's words, on record, set the record straight. In his sermon, "The Tribulation and the Church," he mentions that he *used* to believe in a pretribulation rapture.[3] It is important to recognize that even Walter Martin can change his mind over time. Also, as noted before, he emphatically taught that *the church is the Israel of God*, but that Jews can be grafted into that same tree *if they turn to Christ*. His godly teaching is part of the legacy he left us.

Again, this is not merely a family's difference of opinion. Christian love speaks the truth no matter what the cost. If we only tell one another what we *want* to hear, we have failed to love as Christ loves us and have disobeyed the calling on our lives to honor Christ above all else.

Hank Hanegraaff and Walter Martin have presented their eschatological views to the world "with gentleness and respect." It is not surprising that CRI's presidents have both been called anti-Semitic by Christians and unbelievers alike. This accusation, however, could not be further from the truth. Both leaders have demonstrated their love and compassion toward *all* who need to come to a saving knowledge of Jesus Christ.

---

[3] WalterMartinJude3, "1–6 Dr. Walter Martin: The Tribulation & the Church, PT 1 of 6," YouTube audio clip, 10:00, published February 21, 2010, https://www.youtube.com/watch?v=SA_rEAX0aeE.

12

DR. JOHN WARWICK MONTGOMERY

Another gifted brother in Christ that my father loved is Dr. John Warwick Montgomery. I met him in my childhood. I remember playing with his youngest daughter Kathy as he and his wife visited with my parents at our home in Oakland, New Jersey. Dr. Montgomery and Walter Martin were close friends. Watching them interact at family gatherings was entertaining. They were hilarious. I'd never seen my father laugh as hard as he did during these otherwise uneventful gatherings. I always enjoyed seeing this side of my father. He laughed easily with our family, but these exchanges with Dr. Montgomery were particularly memorable. I recall my father speaking highly of this extremely gifted and accomplished man, on many occasions. Most importantly, Dr. Montgomery has helped equip the body of Christ in significant ways.

At our request, Dr. Montgomery was kind enough, years back, to send Rick and me this exclusive tribute of his friend and brother in Christ, Walter Martin:

> Walter Martin, without exaggeration, has been my dearest friend. Even more than decades since his death, I miss him as much as ever. When I arrive at the heavenly check-in desk (where MAC computers will assure correct results), I intend to locate him right away.
>
> Why Walter? Well, he always referred to me (second and third person) as "Great One" — but I trust that this is not the basis of my esteem for him. There are in fact a multitude of reasons, some general, some very personal.
>
> Theologically, Walter was one of the few Evangelicals who

could think straight. Prof. Dr. Herman Sasse used to say that the contemporary church has forgotten how to think theologically: Walter always thought theologically; he was the Baptist closer to Lutheran theology I have ever met. This meant that he not only took Scripture with complete seriousness but he also was able to distinguish law from gospel, "recognizing the difference between issues on which salvation depends and those which, though in important in other respects, are peripheral to imparting a saving message to a dying world. Thus, his concern with serious apologetics — the defense of the faith (his personalized license plate simply read Jude 3) — when most of his contemporary Evangelicals were far more interested in pandering to church officialdom and obtaining social acceptance in their denominations. Not so incidentally, my first contact with Walter came about because of the laudatory letter he sent to me following my success against death-of-God advocate, Thomas J. J. Altizer in a public debate at the University of Chicago.

Indeed, Walter was at the opposite pole of everything politically correct, and this doubtless kept him from the fame he deserved. (Walter was never, sadly, as popular as the superficial crew of televangelists and writers of forgettable "devotional" books crowding the shelves of the "Bible bookstores.")

Walter's theology was the classic, unmovable theology of the historic church. At the same time, he embraced every innovation for presenting God's eternal truth to modern society. I assisted him on a very early international conference on theology in Austria, and the Christian Research Institute published my contribution in three languages (Computers, Cultural Change, and the Christ, 1989). Following the conference, Walter persuaded me to accompany him on a mission to obtain contributions for the work of CRI from an Austro-German financial magnate who lived in a castle in the Austrian Alps. The man was crazy as a March hare: he thought that he had succeeded in inventing a perpetual motion machine! On the way back, I said to Walter: "That is the last time I ever accompany you on a fundraising expedition." We laughed about this again and again as we traveled the German Autobahn.

Along with his uncompromising theology, Walter had a gigantic heart and was easily hurt. A Pharisaic Bible seminary president in Oregon unilaterally tried to cancel a talk Walter was to give at a major session of the Council on Bible Inerrancy because Walter had been divorced and remarried. I weighed in successfully on that one, having recognized the biblical and Reformation difference between legitimate biblical "causes" of divorce and illegitimate divorce on other grounds. Of course, the fundamentalist critic had no clue as to the historic theological distinction between allowable (though unfortunate) biblical divorce and divorce as such. It cut me to the heart to see Walter suffer from such treatment. And when I myself had problems, Walter was — and immediately — always there. After Walter, the mold was thrown away. I return to where I began: I long to see him again, and, on the basis of God's firm promise, I know that I shall." —John Warwick Montgomery[1]

Dr. Montgomery — staunchly pro-life — endorsed my first (pro-life) book, *Rescue Me*, that Rick and I published a few years ago. Pro-life projects are usually rejected by publishers even when you have a bestselling author as I did, (Hank Hanegraaff) endorsing your book. With fear and trembling, I sent Dr. Montgomery a copy, asking him to consider an endorsement, mindful of the fact that he is an attorney, an accomplished author, and is Emeritus Professor at the University of Bedfordshire, England. No pressure. To my delight, he loved *Rescue Me*. I mention this not to promote myself but to promote the first book I believe the Lord called me to write. If mentioning it will raise more awareness of this unique ministry tool for families, and more children's lives can be saved, it is well worth doing so. I have learned that, for the sake of the unborn little ones threatened by abortion, Christians must take every opportunity that could help them be able to live the life God gave them. No one can do everything, *but we all can do something*. It is critical to pull out all of the stops and to defend the most defenseless among us. If you don't know what to do, financially support a pro-life ministry that does. And above all, pray for the children.

Dr. Montgomery's endorsement of *Rescue Me*:

> Christian fiction generally sets the children's teeth on edge, owing to its substitution of moralism and do-goodishness for the biblical gospel. And the authors, whatever their theology, more than often than not *cannot write*. Cindee Morgan is a wonderful exception on both counts. *Immediately order this book for your teenager* — and for yourself (as long as you haven't repressed the child within you). And should you be a right-to-lifer — we trust that, as a Christian believer you couldn't be otherwise — this is the book you always wanted.

---

[1] This tribute does not represent Dr. Montgomery's views on any particular church. It is included in loving memory of Cindee Martin Morgan's father and the memorable friendship the two men shared. To learn more about John Warwick Montgomery, see https://www.jwm.christendom.co.uk and https://www.apologeticsacademy.eu.

Cindee's late father and my dear friend Walter R. Martin will be celebrating in heaven on publication day.

— Dr John Warwick Montgomery, Professor emeritus, University of Bedfordshire, England, Distinguish Professor of Philosophy, Concordia University, Wisconsin

It is evident the Lord provided great pro-life men of God — Dr. Montgomery, Hank Hanegraaff, Rolley Haggard, Chris Arnzen, and others — to enable *Rescue Me* to have far greater exposure for the sake of those who have no voice. These men publicly continue to defend the lives of the unborn in the face of a world that has forgotten them.

Hank has interviewed me several times through the years and featured my first pro-life song, "Fearfully and Wonderfully Made," a number of occasions on the *Bible Answer Man* program. CRI also shared our video featuring my pro-life song, "Who Will Save the Little Ones?" God has used both of these as a voice for the unborn by way of YouTube and other venues. I am proud of CRI for defending the most vulnerable among us while not condemning those who have made the tragic choice to participate in an abortion. There is pardon for us all at the foot of the cross. "There is none righteous" (Romans 3:10).

The Bible Answer Man
Walter Martin and Hank Hanegraaff

Walter Martin with friends John Ankerberg and his wife, Darlene.

Walter Martin and his wife Darlene, at their home, with Everett and Gladys Jacobson in San Juan Capistrano. 1988.

Rick and I with uncle Everett and aunt Gladys at my father's home. 1988.

My father babysitting my daughter Stacie's Cabbage Patch doll.

Grandad Martin with granddaughters Stacie, Sharon and Richelle in Arizona. 1988.

My father giving us a grand tour of CRI's newest facility in Irvine, California. 1989.

Walter Martin making a quick stop, with granddaughter Sharon in tow, at Research Coordinator Dan Schlesinger's office at CRI.

Walter Martin and his wife Darlene with Hank and Kathy Hanegraaff.

A dear brother in Christ gifted my father with this inspiring caricature based on I Timothy 6:12.

My sister Debbie and I at our father's grave.

Elliot and Corinne Miller and I at the funeral of Everett Jacobson in West Palm Beach, Florida. 2007.

The Bible Answer Man
Walter Martin and Hank Hanegraaff

Rick and I on a Sovereign Group Leader Caribbean Cruise with Hank Hanegraaff and a number of other Christian leaders. 2010.

Fellowshipping with Hank and Kathy Hanegraaff during one of our evenings aboard the ship.

Hank Hanegraaff and I standing in front of the ship, the MSC Poesia.

The Bible Answer Man
Walter Martin and Hank Hanegraaff

Founder and former President of the Christian Research Institute (CRI), and the original *Bible Answer Man*, Walter Martin.

The *Bible Answer Man* studio in Charlotte, North Carolina.

President of the Christian Research Institute (CRI) and host of the *Bible Answer Man* program, Hank Hanegraaff.

The Bible Answer Man
Walter Martin and Hank Hanegraaff

13

HANK HANEGRAAFF AND THE GREEK ORTHODOX CHURCH

There was never a dull moment when Walter Martin was on the air, nor is there one when Hank answers questions and interviews guests on the *Bible Answer Man* broadcast and on *Hank Unplugged*. There have been many notable guests over the years, all contributing their expertise in many areas. One guest in the late '90s was Judge Robert Bork. Hank highly esteemed him, once saying, he is a "judicial genius, and a prophet — his writing, including one of my all-time favorite books, *Slouching Towards Gomorrah: Modern Liberalism and American Decline*, set forth precisely what we see happening in America today. And Bork with his sharp wit and smoker's cough was quite a character, too."[1]

Hank describes a memorable interview with Phillip E. Johnson, describing him as a "brilliant man." He interviewed him multiple times on the *Bible Answer Man* program, calling him "the godfather of the Intelligent Design movement." He is a professor of Law, Emeritus at the University of California, Berkeley School of Law, and once served as law clerk to Chief Justice Earl Warren. Johnson authored *Darwin on Trial* and other books, demonstrating, in Hank's opinion, "evolution is propped up more by naturalistic philosophy than by the scientific evidence." Hank considers Professor Johnson "a force of nature," stating that "his work is among the most important of the late twentieth century."[2] I wholeheartedly agree.

A timely guest Hank's had on the *Bible Answer Man* Broadcast, and now the *Hank Unplugged* podcast (whom he's had on the broadcast more times

---

[1] This was from a personal email to the author from Hank Hanegraaff.
[2] This was from a personal email to the author from Hank Hanegraaff.

than any other) is Joe Dallas. Hank has stated many times, and it's true, that "no one understands the subject of sexual purity better than Joe Dallas. And in our post-truth, post-Christian culture, Joe's proclamation and defense of the essential biblical sexual ethic cannot be over emphasized."[3]

There have been many great guests on the *Bible Answer Man* Broadcast, including Lee Strobel, Jack Countryman, Dr. Paul Nelson, and many more.

I asked Hank what motivated him to create CRI's riveting *Hank Unplugged* podcast, an interesting new addition to CRI's ministry. Hank briefly explained how this came about:

> I'd been doing the *Bible Answer Man* broadcast for nearly three decades, and I felt I needed another medium in which I could, as it were, go off the grid — to range further, to dive deeper into issues of interest to thinking people, Christians and non-Christians alike. It's given me an opportunity to dialogue with some of my closest friends, brightest minds, and best thinkers, the most interesting people in the world for engaging, free-flowing, interactive conversations on vital issues facing the world today. In the podcast, I leave the studio, as it were, and welcome listeners into my study for a far more personal perspective on matters of life and truth — I use the word "unplugged" because the podcast reflects the intense, informal conversations on essential issues my wife, family, and close friends are familiar with. Ultimately, as with the *Bible Answer Man* Broadcast, the podcast exists to equip Christians to impact the world for Christ, to become cultural change agents and initiators, as opposed to being cultural conformists and imitators.

This new addition to CRI has blessed the body of Christ. Hank is always coming up with new ways to reach the lost and to equip Christians with tools to help them share the truth of the gospel. This is one of the main reasons Walter Martin chose him to lead CRI. The *Bible Answer Man* Broadcast has helped an untold number of people to come to know the gospel of Jesus Christ. It has equipped millions to know how to defend their faith. For nearly sixty years, CRI has given tremendous glory to God.

When Hank Hanegraaff was diagnosed with stage 4 mantle cell lymphoma, our hearts sunk. We quickly researched this form of cancer and prayed there was a cure or a medical path to remission. On the heels of learning of Hank's illness, we found out he'd joined the Greek Orthodox Church. As the Christian media shared this breaking news, some Evangelicals experienced a theological cardiac arrest — *I was one of them*. I took my

---

[3] This was from a personal email to the author from Hank Hanegraaff.

concerns directly to Hank, and he graciously answered my questions. Rick and I privately asked some for prayer, as we were uncertain how Hank's cancer and his leaving Protestantism would impact CRI. People flocked to my Facebook page seeking answers both publicly and privately. Most were kind, but some condemned Hank, accused him of leaving the faith, and some even mocked him as an apostate. Rick and I believe Hank is a brother in Christ, and we never had that concern. This new development, however, catapulted us through the doctrinal door of this ancient church to a place we'd never been before. Whether we agreed with Hank becoming Greek Orthodox or not, we were determined to understand *why* he had made this decision. We also began taking a closer look at the church fathers, church history, Martin Luther, C. S. Lewis, Walter Martin, and other men of God.

As Rick and I read about Greek Orthodoxy and listened to videos about this Church on YouTube, it soon became evident there were many misunderstandings and some people misrepresenting it. Secondly, they were not correctly communicating to people what *Hank* himself believes. Some seemed well meaning, but others were anything but; shameful assumptions were made. There were those who theologically stoned Hank, assuming the worst possible conclusions and presenting them as fact. A few greatly *increased* their efforts to harm CRI. In the well-balanced articles by the *Christian Post*, I defended Hank as a brother in Jesus Christ.

To have a glimpse of what Hank endured, we must first put ourselves in his shoes. Imagine, for a moment, you as a Protestant are being defined theologically to the world by people who don't even know you. The Protestant Church is so splintered we can't possibly define each other without knowing one another personally. Americanized Christianity can be consumed in every church around us. So much of it is *not* what the church once was. The Protestant church is just as corrupt as churches of old. Homosexuality and abortion are approved of, participated in, and promoted by many. Some have come to believe that you no longer have to confess your sins to God to be forgiven. Luther is esteemed, in our times, because of the Reformation. Reform *was* needed in the Catholic Church, but the Reformation was not the beginning of Christianity; it was an effort to defend it. As my father once said, "In the entire history of the church, God raises up apostles, in the beginning prophets, and then the church fathers. Then, after them, the Reformers, and so forth. What was the purpose? It was to bring the church back to the path she deviated from, theologically. Now, we are deviate in a massive way today."[4]

---

[4] Cindee Martin Morgan, "1/2 Walter Martin/TBN (Trinity Broadcasting Network) 1-2" YouTube video, 23:54, published July 17, 2011, https://www.youtube.com/watch?v=l8xAVR1sG0I.

Luther remained *quite* Catholic throughout his life and didn't reject many things that most Protestant churches reject today. It was *not* his desire to leave the Catholic Church. He set out to reform it but instead found himself excommunicated. Certain things Luther espoused caused fissures and divisions within the Protestant movement, yet God used him to bring about needed reform.

Martin Luther was hardly opposed to the Greek Orthodox Church; the average Christian probably is not aware of this. *Christianity Today* spotlighted this fact in an article entitled "What Did the Reformers Think about the Eastern Orthodox Church?"[5]

What many don't realize is that Hank is being condemned for believing some of the *same things* Martin Luther believed and taught until his death. Worse yet, Hank is accused of things he *does not believe*. Why is one an Icon of the Reformation and the other rejected by some as an apostate? I believe it's because so many are unaware of church history and what our heroes of the faith actually believed. In some cases, Christians simply choose to ignore ancient beliefs that contradict their own.

J. C. Ryle's profound sermon "The True Church" helps to clarify this question. In his message, he states:

> The Church of our text is no material building. It is no temple made with hands, of wood, or brick, or stone, or marble. It is a company of men and women. It is no particular visible Church on earth. It is not the Eastern Church or the Western Church. It is not the Church of England, or the Church of Scotland — much less is it the Church of Rome. The Church of our text is one that makes far less show in the eyes of man, but is of far more importance in the eyes of God.
>
> The Church of our text is made up of all true believers in the Lord Jesus Christ. It comprehends all who have repented of sin, and fled to Christ by faith, and been made new creatures in Him. It comprises all God's elect, all who have received God's grace, all who have been washed in Christ's blood, all who have been clothed in Christ's righteousness, all who have been born again and sanctified by Christ's Spirit. All such, of every nation, and people, and tongue, compose the Church of our text. This is the body of Christ. This is the flock of Christ. This is the bride. This is the Lamb's wife. This is the Church on the rock.

---

[5] The Editors, "What Did the Reformers Think about the Eastern Orthodox Church?," *Christianity Today*, August 8, 2008, https://www.christianitytoday.com/history/2008/august/what-did-reformers-think-about-eastern-orthodox-church.html.

> The members of this Church do not all worship God in the same way or use the same form of government. Our own 34th Article declares, "It is not necessary that ceremonies should be in all places one and alike." But they all worship with one heart. They are all led by one Spirit. They are all really and truly holy. They can all say "Alleluia," and they can all reply "Amen."[6]

Greek Orthodoxy is *not* Catholicism, and yet it has been misrepresented as a light form of it. A serious study of both demonstrates they are two distinct Churches. Both contain the core doctrine of Christianity, as does the Protestant Church. These labels save no one eternally but do separate us from the cults. What is true is we will only be saved *if* we *know Jesus Christ* as Lord and Savior. We must *confess our sins, hold fast the core doctrine* of Christianity, *love as Christ loves us,* and *obey the Word of God.* The gospel was handed down through the ages by the power of God. It was preserved not because of men but in spite of men, with the Lord directing its path. It was corrupted every step of the way, as sinful men deciphered it, yet God protected what is necessary for his children to be saved.

What convinced Hank to choose Greek Orthodoxy was his belief in Christ's presence in the Eucharist. Martin Luther believed this ancient teaching, yet Hank is demonized for believing it also. Luther had no intention of throwing the baby out with the bathwater in terms of doctrine he believed to be sound. In a real sense, the modern churches pay no mind to the established traditions and beliefs of the ancient church. What ancient orthodox churches have done for *two thousand years* may, at times, sound evil to us. How do some of us respond? We reject what we don't understand.

Charles Spurgeon, in his day, contended with the seeds of dispensationalism being planted and believed it contradicted the Bible. In our day, this teaching has grown by leaps and bounds, yet long ago it was frowned upon.

Christians, through the ages, have been arguing and fighting about doctrine that is *not* essential to salvation. John Calvin thought it was righteous to burn people at the stake, and yet many esteem him, quote him, and don't dwell on his darkest sins (myself included). Had some of us lived in his time, we would have recognized the evil being done to others (God willing) and have resisted it.

In America, we are not allowed to murder (unless it's innocent life in the womb or sometimes criminals), so it's reputations we choose to burn instead. If a professed believer in Jesus Christ does not conform to our way of

---

[6] J. C. Ryle, "The True Church," Virtue Online, https://www.virtueonline.org/true-church-jc-ryle.

thinking — apart from the essentials — we demonize them and, in doing so, have gained nothing profitable, because we have failed to show the love and mercy we receive from the Lord *every single day*.

We are warned, in 1 Corinthians 13, "Though I speak with the tongues of men and of angels, but have not love, I have become as sounding brass or a clanging cymbal....it profits me nothing." The passage goes on to carefully define the kind of love we are to extend to those around us. I have heard many Christians claim they have the right to act like Jesus did in Matthew, chapter 21, where Jesus flipped tables and strongly rebuked the money changers in the temple. We are not given permission to emulate that level of confrontation. *Jesus is God.* The type of love He demonstrated in the temple was love that perfectly displayed His judgment, righteous indignation and correction. We are *not* God and are given a well-defined code of conduct throughout Scripture. Do we oppose what we perceive as error? Yes, but when we correct someone, as Scripture warns, we better have the "plank" of error out of our own eye first (Matthew 7:5) and humbly do it with gentleness and respect.

C. S. Lewis, who is regarded by many as the greatest apologist of the twentieth century, sought to bring churches together who believed the essentials of Christianity. He spoke against the divisions and factions that have always plagued the church. Lewis was Anglican yet was impressed with Greek Orthodoxy, still relatively new to America. Lewis's biographer explained that Lewis preferred the Greek Orthodox liturgy to Protestant or Roman Catholic liturgies.[7]

Lewis highly esteemed Greek Orthodox liturgy and puts this Church, the Protestant Church, and Roman Catholic Church in the category of *Christianity*. I am certain that many, like this book's author, had no idea this is what Lewis thought. Once again, we esteem him but overlook or are unaware of everything he believed. Rick and I know someone who publicly stated that C. S. Lewis would be "turning over in his grave" regarding Hank's church choice. As my father used to say — and I say it now in love — "they have not done their homework."

Hank Hanegraaff joined a godly Greek Orthodox Church and has done his homework. Like C. S. Lewis, he sees the value in its liturgy — the heart and soul of a church — and appreciates the reverence for the Eucharist that he believes is lacking in the Protestant Church.

In Hank's church, he met people alive for Jesus Christ; he also met people who are spiritual dead men walking. Hank would be the first to tell you that he believes many people are lost in the Greek Orthodox Church. He would also tell you how he believes many are lost in both the Protestant and

---

[7] "C. S. Lewis," Orthodox Wiki, https://orthodoxwiki.org/C._S._Lewis.

in the Catholic denominations, as well. Scripture emphasizes how the wheat grows with the tares.

Hank Hanegraaff is not a traitor to the faith. He has written more than twenty biblical books and is a best-selling, award-winning author. While being a successful writer doesn't make you a Christian, his numerous books encapsulate the gospel of Jesus Christ. There is a simple reason for this: Hank loves the Lord! Has Hank sinned and fallen short of the glory of God? Has he done things his heart grieves over, and for which he has sought forgiveness? I am certain of this. The man that Rick and I know is a flawed man, like every believer saved by the mercy of God. As the apostle Paul cried out, "Wretched man that I am! Who will deliver me from this body of death?" (Romans 7:24).

Franklin Graham, as did his father, seeks to bring Christian churches together with core Christian beliefs. A staff writer for the *Indianapolis Star*, Judith Cebula, who interviewed Franklin Graham many years ago, stated in her article "Keeping It Simple, Safe Keeps Graham on High" that "During [Billy] Graham's rise to prominence in the 1950's, he became a pioneer in ecumenism. He broke rank with many fundamentalists by reaching out to Catholics and mainline Protestants. In 1951, he launched a 10-year dialogue with the Catholic cardinal of Boston. And in 1957, he sought support from the liberal Protestant Council of Churches for his legendary 16-week New York Crusade." She adds, "Franklin Graham believes that risk [of inclusiveness] was one of the smartest things his father ever did. He has followed in those footsteps at his own revivals and as president of Samaritan's Purse, a worldwide Christian relief organization." Franklin Graham stated, "In the early years, up in Boston, the Catholic church got behind my father's crusade. That was a first. It took back many Protestants. They didn't know how to handle it, but it set the example. If Billy Graham is willing to work with everybody, then maybe we should too."[8]

These two men of God had/have the mindset of C. S. Lewis. The Billy Graham Association has stood by persecuted Christians around the globe, and have rallied the Protestant, Greek Orthodox, and Catholic Churches around critical issues facing the church today. This is profoundly biblical.

Walter Martin respected the Grahams, C. S. Lewis, and Hank Hanegraaff. He believed much as they did; the ministry of CRI reflects this both during my father's life and since he positioned Hank to lead CRI. Hank did a powerful interview on *Hank Unplugged* with Anne Graham Lotz, Billy Graham's daughter.

---

[8] Judith Cebula, "Keeping It Simple, Safe Keeps Graham on High: Avoiding Divisive Issues, Crusader Has Reached 210 Million but Left Some Activists Disappointed," *Indianapolis Star*, June 3, 1999.

Chuck Colson and many others have sought to bring unity to the body of Christ. Tony Perkins, founder of the Family Research Council, has been a voice for persecuted Christians, acknowledging the suffering of our brothers and sisters in Christ in a Fox Video entitled "Targeting of Christians."[9] Without a doubt, Tony Perkins recognizes the Catholic and Greek Orthodox churches as being Christian.

In supporting one another, no one denies our theological differences. Mark Ross, John R. de Witt Professor of Systematic Theology and director of the Institute for Reformed Worship at Erskine Theological Seminary, eloquently adds biblical food for thought, regarding biblical love and unity, in an insightful article: "In essentials Unity, In Non-Essentials Liberty, In All Things Charity: We cannot simply reduce the number of doctrines to be taught and believed to what we can all accept as important and ignore the rest. Movement in that direction always seems to lose its brakes and eventually nothing distinctive of Christianity remains. But neither can we lock ourselves up in very small groups with maximal agreement on doctrine and morals, and then separate from others and refuse to acknowledge as Christians those who do not embrace all our distinctives."[10]

The Evangelical, Catholic, and Greek Orthodox Churches, warts and all, do not oppose Christianity. None have denied the true Jesus, for example, as the cults have done. They haven't declared themselves sinless, professed they are gods, or promoted a satanic gospel written on golden plates.

When all is said and done, God alone decides who belongs to Him in the end, and who does not. He said he will have His angels separate the wheat from the tares, before the wheat march off to glory, and the tares descend to hell. Until we lie cold in our graves, God is not finished yet.

We must pray for the lost, let them know they need a Savior, and declare the truth of the gospel in love. We must examine fruit in our lives, daily, and examine the fruit of others. We must expose and oppose evil. We must run the race God has set before us. But, as the Word of God teaches, we *must allow* the wheat to grow with the tares. We are not to condemn one another but instead pray for each other, recognizing that we ourselves were once lost. I must confess that after witnessing the persecution of our brother in Christ, Hank Hanegraaff, I want only to be known as a child of God. Our church choice does not save us. We are saved by the power of God "who works in

---

[9] Fox Video, http://www.frc.org/get.cfm?c=PLAY_MEDIA&playItem=MD17D03.

[10] Mark Ross, "In Essentials Unity, In Non-Essentials Liberty, In All Things Charity," Ligonier Ministries, September 9, 2012, https://www.ligonier.org/learn/articles/essentials-unity-non-essentials-liberty-all-things/.

you both to will and to do for His good pleasure" (Philippians 2:13).

14

CALLED TO SUFFER

"The Spirit Himself bears witness with our spirit that we are children of God, and if children, then heirs — heirs of God and joint heirs with Christ, if indeed we suffer with Him, that we may also be glorified together." (Romans 8:16–17)

I began writing this book in January of 2018. Little did I realize the kind of year Rick and I would face. We have noticed that every time the Lord gives us something major to accomplish for Him, we experience severe trials. During this project, two of our dearest friends died. In addition, Rick and I were hit by one of the largest semi-trucks we have ever seen. By the mercy of God, we were unharmed. One evening, I almost choked to death on a piece of steak; Rick had to perform the Heimlich maneuver on me — three times — before I could breathe. He saved my life. I was painfully aware that, during my childhood, one of my father's friends had choked to death on a piece of steak, and I praise God for sparing my family this grief. Nothing, however, could prepare us for the trial that was just around the bend.

I was busy wrapping up this book when my precious husband had a major stroke. The earthquake that hit our family felt like a 10.0 in magnitude.

Rick and I were preparing to leave for CRI's former editor-in-chief's Elliot Miller's memorial service, in California, and to celebrate our thirty-sixth wedding anniversary. We had just finished lunch on August 12. Rick and I were having a conversation about this book. I asked him a question, which he didn't answer completely right. I asked it again. Rick looked at me a bit puzzled and said very slowly, "I – don't – know – how – to – answer – you."

We thought he'd had a TIA (Transient Ischemic Attack); everything else about Rick seemed fine, and he began to speak again more normally. We got ready to drive to the emergency room to have Rick checked out. Our assumption that this was a mini-stroke was short lived. As Rick got up from the couch to leave, he almost fell over. We made the mistake of not calling an ambulance, as Rick strongly insisted it wasn't needed. We both regret our decision to not do so, because we later learned that is the wisest course of action under these circumstances. With hearts pounding, our oldest daughter Stacie drove us to the hospital.

Instead of preparing for a trip to California, Rick and I were praying the Lord would not take him home to heaven.

Although sharp minded, he had brain fog. His face soon fell on one side. We stormed the gates of heaven and asked everyone we knew to do so as well. After three terrifying nights in the ICU, Rick turned a corner and was admitted into the rehabilitation side of the hospital. We were elated. The next morning, however, we were stunned to find out that the whole right side of his body didn't work. Doctors were concerned he may have had another stroke. Due to increased hospital emergencies that day, Rick could not get an MRI until late that evening. The following afternoon, God brought the news that we had been waiting for; Rick had not had another stroke. Praise God.

As the days passed, my husband grew stronger, and we celebrated our anniversary in his hospital room. It was the first night we hadn't slept under the same roof on this special day. It didn't matter. I was so thankful to the Lord that my husband and the father of my children was on the road to recovery. He had a life-threatening stroke, and God had spared him.

God surrounded us with an enormous amount of support, especially during this season. We asked for prayer the Lord would keep Rick safe in every way possible and that the peace that passes all understanding would fill our hearts.

Within a week's time, Rick was walking again with assistance. God sustained our family as we cheered him on in his recovery. Although his right leg was wobbly, he pressed on, determined to be whole again. His right arm and hand slowly began to wake up, too. After a month in the hospital, God brought my husband home to me, to our four daughters, to our grandchildren, and to our Schnoodle puppy, Brinkley, who was lost without him. While rehab continues to this day, we praise the Lord for his mercies that are new every morning. This trial is the hardest our family has ever endured. We recognize, though, that as children of God we will not be spared suffering. As J. C. Ryle profoundly stated:

> All the sons of God take part in suffering with Christ.....They have trials, troubles, and afflictions to go through for the Gospel's sake. They have trials from the *world*, trials from the flesh, and trials from the devil.... They have sharp trials from *relations* and *friends* —

hard words, hard treatment, and hard judgment. They have trials in the matter of *character*: slander, misrepresentation, mockery, insinuation of false motives — all these often rain thick upon them.... Some of them suffer more, and some less. Some of them suffer in one way, and some in another. God *measures out their portions* like a wise physician and cannot err.... Suffering is the *diet* of the Lord's family. Suffering is a part of the process by which the sons of God are *sanctified*. They are *chastened* to wean them from the world and make them partakers of God's holiness. The Captain of their salvation was 'made perfect through suffering,' and so are they. (Hebrews 2:10; 12:10)....The Bridegroom was a *man of sorrows*. The Bride must not be a *woman of pleasures* and unacquainted with grief. Blessed are those who mourn![1]

The current president of CRI has suffered tremendous trial. Hank has battled stage 4 cancer while enduring some members in the body of Christ insisting that he is an apostate. Would Walter Martin have thought so? It is my firmly held conviction that he would not have judged him so harshly. My father's decision to make Hank his right-hand man at CRI, shortly before he died, was wise and well thought out. Additionally, Walter Martin was compassionate and understood that Christians can have major differences. His sermons, writings, and *Bible Answer Man* program demonstrated that he was much like C. S. Lewis, who also believed that the core doctrine of Christianity historically exists in the Protestant, Greek Orthodox, and the Catholic church. Walter Martin used to tell Christians, "Don't major in the minors."

My father taught me that it is a relationship with our Lord Jesus Christ that is what saves us. His life demonstrated to me that "I dare not trust the sweetest frame, but wholly lean on Jesus' name." For Walter Martin to condemn Hank as a heretic would mean he would have to condemn Martin Luther and countless others who have gone before us. Unbelievers need to see Christians unite on the essentials of our faith and stop seeking each other's destruction. May God help us extend the same mercy to our brothers and sisters in Christ we've been so freely given.

While preparing this book for publication, we received news that Hank Hanegraaff's cancer is in remission. *The Christian Post* and many other news outlets helped spread the miracle.[2] Sadly, the remission was short lived; the

---

[1] J. C. Ryle, *Practical Religion* (London: Charles Murray, 1900), 418–19, emphasis in original.
[2] https://www.christianpost.com/news/bible-answer-man-hank-hanegraaffs-cancer-in-remission-gods-grace.html.

tumors have returned. Hank's doctors continue to explore ways to fight for the life of this dear warrior of the cross.

Please pray for the Christian Research Institute. It has survived treacherous theological seas both in Walter Martin's day and since Hank Hanegraaff has been president. Please join us in praying that some who have removed the *Bible Answer Man* program from their networks would yet again recognize the value of this dynamic ministry.

Hank has been judged in a way none of us would want to be judged and prevented, in a limited sense, from sharing the gospel of Jesus Christ. If the *Bible Answer Man* and CRI have been a blessing in your life, write the radio stations who have censored one of the greatest apologetic ministries the church and America has ever known — please do so for the sake of the gospel. The Lord has blessed the body of Christ with a vital ministry that faithfully shines the light of the gospel into a dark world that desperately needs a Savior. As my grandmother taught me to pray as a small child, "God bless CRI and all of its efforts" for God's glory and the extension of His Kingdom.

APPENDIX

CRI PRESIDENT HANK HANEGRAAFF: AN IN-DEPTH INTERVIEW

CRI's presidents are more similar than many realize. Walter Martin and Hank Hanegraaff both spoke out against the prosperity gospel — the Faith Movement. Hank's best-selling book *Christianity in Crisis: 21st Century* powerfully equips the body of Christ with reasons why they should flee from the dangerous teaching that you can name-and-claim your destiny, essentially writing your own Christian journey. There are people who live in fear of saying even one negative word. They're afraid to confess out loud they are sick, out of concern that *their very words* will make them sicker. They have been taught if they ask the Lord to heal them, and He doesn't, they don't have enough faith. They believe the lie God wants every child of God to be healthy and wealthy and have clung to other false teachings as well. Both CRI's presidents faithfully sought to expose these heresies that have infiltrated the Evangelical Church.

In addition, both have end times views that are out of step with many modern churches. Both men have a robust understanding of libertarian freedom of the will. Both of CRI's presidents highly esteem C. S. Lewis. Each has majorly helped to equip the body of Christ with important resources through CRI and the CHRISTIAN RESEARCH JOURNAL. Hank's book *Muslim* is extremely timely and would have been a book my father most likely would have written too, had Islam been the threat it is to the civilized world today. Having the blessing of knowing these gifted warriors of the cross, it is obvious to me how God himself orchestrated the path of this ministry; God

The Bible Answer Man
Walter Martin and Hank Hanegraaff

is in control.

The following is a lightly edited transcript of my in-depth interview with our brother in Christ, Hank Hanegraaff (recorded August 7, 2018):[1]

HANK: Hey, Cindee.

CINDEE: Hi, Hank. How are you doing?

HANK: I'm doing great.

CINDEE: Thank you so much for being willing to sit down with me like this. This is so kind of you. We're kind of switching chairs today, aren't we?

HANK: Absolutely. Yes, I get to be interviewed.

CINDEE: How are you feeling, first off?

HANK: Well, I feel great. I just flew in from Southern California last night. I've got a little jet lag going on, but not too bad.

CINDEE: Good. OK, well, let's get started. My first question I most wanted to hear more details about is what was that moment you turned to Jesus Christ? What was the defining moment for you when you knew you needed a Savior, you were lost, and you had that feeling He is God?

HANK: Well, it's a long story. I actually grew up in a Christian home. I was born in Holland. I grew up in the Christian Reformed Church and was in that context for *many* years of my life. I was going to church and doing all the things that Christians do: reading the Bible as a discipline, learning to memorize the catechism, being *faithful* in going to church, and all these kinds of things were part and parcel to my growing-up years. As I grew older, particularly in my teenage years, I started questioning the Christian faith, particularly questioning the hard determinism that I was being taught, that God creates people who are doomed from the womb to certain destruction. I was very conflicted by the hard determinism and asked my parents questions, my pastors, and my Christian schoolteachers because I went to

---

[1] This interview can be heard online also; *Hank Unplugged* podcast, episode 75, "A Personal Look at Hank's Journey with Cindee Martin Morgan," *Bible Answer Man* YouTube video, 1:52:30, published January 30, 2019, https://www.youtube.com/watch?v=R5Lqd5fJ9JQ.

Christian schools. I didn't get satisfying answers, and so I started to drift away from the Christian faith.

And, it wasn't just that. It was many other questions that I was asking, and of course this was, you know, a very transitional time not only for me personally but also for the country. We immigrated first to Canada when I was three and then to the United States when I was fourteen, 1964. The year of Berkeley and the Beatles. The year Cassius Clay took the Muslim moniker Mohammad Ali. The year of the Civil Rights Bill and Joan Baez. That was the year after the assassination — we were still grieving the assassination of J.F.K. Bob Dylan — "The Times They Are A-Changin'," you know — so it was a tremendous time of transition that was taking place, and here I was, a new American, newly in America. At that time, my questions became more and more intense. Even at age fourteen, I thought, "You know what, I don't believe in God. I don't really believe in God. I can't believe in the God that I've been brought up to believe in. I can't get satisfying answers." After a while, I kind of moved off into what I would call practical atheism. I kept sort of being drawn back into the Christian faith, but for all practical purposes, I was an atheist. I was living as though there was no such thing as God. So, I drifted in and out of spirituality during that time.

It didn't really change until I was twenty-nine years of age when three people from a local church — happened to be Coral Ridge Presbyterian Church — came and they were going to visit someone who had visited the church, and they knocked on my door instead. They invited me to go to a creation/evolution seminar, and that started me looking at the issue of origins; and that led me into asking, if God created the universe, then did that God reveal himself in time and space and resurrection? Is it logical to believe in the resurrection of Jesus Christ? And finally, to look at the validity of the Bible. Is it a reliable authority? So, at that time (it was 1979), I came to faith in Christ.

Again, I came out of a church background, but then I realized, wow, I had just given up one kind of hard determinism for another, because in atheism you believe that everything is controlled by genetics and brain chemistry — all the physical facts — we're fatalistically determined by our genetics, and so forth. So, it was at that time, after searching those three great apologetics issues, looking at the issues of origins, resurrection, and the authority of Scripture, I found myself on my knees asking Jesus Christ to be Lord and Savior of my life, in a very intentional way. I became a member of Coral Ridge Presbyterian Church. I learned how to share my faith through Evangelism Explosion, and the rest, as they say, is history.

CINDEE: As you were talking about your background growing up — your father was a pastor, of course, in the Reformed faith — I couldn't help but think of my own father and the theological talks I had with him. I didn't always agree with him, and it made me think about his responses to that. What was it like having dialogues with your father during the time you weren't saved, when you had all these questions? How hard on your father was that? What kind of dialogue did you have with your father?

HANK: Well, we had a lot of conversations. Some of them positive, some of them negative. On a positive note, I remember during the time we had the Cuban missile crisis, laying on the couch and trembling in terror because at that time there was the possibility that the world was going to go up in a nuclear holocaust. I had been in church listening to my dad preach, and my dad was preaching on the apostle Paul, in Romans. I don't remember the exact context, but I remember as a young boy listening. My dad was using the word *Paulus*, preaching in Dutch, actually, and as I was listening to the sermon, I thought I blasphemed the Holy Spirit — I thought I'd committed an unforgivable sin. Just in my mind. So, when the Cuban missile crisis happened, I thought, wow, I have committed an unforgivable sin. The world's going to go up in a nuclear holocaust, I'm going to go to hell forever, and I was trembling in fear.

My dad came into the living room and he said to me, "What's wrong?"

I divulged to him that during one of his sermons, I committed the blasphemy of the Holy Spirit.

He smiled at me and said, "If you had committed the blasphemy of the Holy Spirit, you wouldn't be trembling right now; you wouldn't be worried about it."

That was a very edifying time, and to this day, I have used that illustration when people call me on the radio and say, "I think I've committed the blasphemy of the Holy Spirit." I say, "Well, that's not an act. The blasphemy of the Holy Spirit is a continuous, willful, ongoing rejection of the goodness and grace of God that could be yours."

CINDEE: Absolutely.

HANK: So, that was a wonderful experience that I had with my dad. My dad taught me so many things that I didn't appreciate when I was growing up. He taught me discipline. He taught me respect, particularly for older people. He taught me integrity. He taught me fidelity. He taught me commitment — that love is not just a feeling; it's a commitment. He modeled how a relationship between a man and woman ought to be. He and my mom — my mom's still alive — were madly in love. They were until my dad went home to be with the Lord in 1997. There were many things that my dad modeled for me. There were times when I appreciated that, and times I didn't *understand* the gift that I had been given. After I became a Christian, I committed my life to the Lord, and I realized what a tremendous background I had received in the church — in discipline — in memorizing the Heidelberg catechism, being a faithful member of the church, and all these kinds of things. So, the things I resented growing up I realized were a tremendous gift.

CINDEE: It was; you had a firm foundation.

HANK: A firm foundation, yes. The reason I give that as context is a lot of times someone says, "I came to Christ when I was twenty-nine years old," but think when they started at twenty-nine, it was a blank slate. No, it wasn't. I had a *deep* well to draw from in terms of my own Christian experience as a result of the context in which I grew up.

CINDEE: Yes. God is working before we know it.

HANK: Absolutely, that's true.

CINDEE: Wow, that is really a precious testimony. How did you meet your wife, Kathy?

HANK: Well, when I committed my life to the Lord, Kathy was deeply involved in Evangelism Explosion, and she became my first trainer. Evangelism Explosion is a worldwide program that was designed to equip Christians not only in classroom training but also in the field — where evangelism is more caught than taught. Kathy was already a trainer, and she invited me into the program, and I became a trainee; she was my first teacher. Kathy taught me how to share my faith, practically, as well as in the actual learning process itself. So, I quickly became a trainer myself — a trainer of trainers — and that was a life-transforming experience, but that's how I met Kathy.

CINDEE: Did it click with you two right away?

HANK: [*laughter*] At first, I was thinking of setting her up with a friend of mine. I remember talking to D. James Kennedy. He counseled us when we decided to start dating. I still remember being in his office, and he looked at me and said, "If you don't marry that girl, you are the dumbest person on the planet."

CINDEE: That is so sweet. So, the rest is history. How long have you been married now?

HANK: We have been married since 1980.

CINDEE: OK, and *twelve* children, right?

HANK: Three adopted and nine natural. Yes.

CINDEE: What inspired you guys to have so many children?

HANK: Well, it's not you guys. It's Kathy.

CINDEE: [*laughs*]

HANK: Every time she got pregnant, I was a little bit upset about it, so she'd find a nice way to tell me she was pregnant again. Again, in retrospect — sort of like I was saying about my parents — I never had any intent to have a large family. Now, in retrospect, when your kids grow up to become your friends, and you get to travel with them, it's just fantastic. So, I'm *very*, *very* grateful that Kathy wanted to have a large family, although at the time, I was kind of thinking, "How am I going to handle one more child?" But, you know that's a great example of how God always provides.

CINDEE: He does. He really does provide, and God had a plan.

HANK: He most certainly did.

CINDEE: He shows you how good that plan is as time moves on.

HANK: That's right.

CINDEE: Whom do you consider your number-one mentor?

HANK: Oh, my goodness.

CINDEE: That's probably going to be tough.

HANK: Yeah, that's a good question.

CINDEE: You're not confined to just one.

HANK: I've had so many great mentors. Your dad was a great mentor to me. You know, he was willing to stand for truth no matter what the cost. I remember so many statements that he made in that regard.

Chuck Colson was a great mentor to me. Early on, R. C. Sproul — who went home to be with the Lord last year — he was a *very* dear friend of mine. When he was back in Ligonier, Pennsylvania, and I was just a brand-new Christian (so this is the early '80s), he would always invite me up to Ligonier, and we would play golf together. He'd come knocking on my little cabin door — they had those cabins out there — and he'd come knocking when the sun came up, and we'd play golf all day. Then we'd go into his driveway, shoot baskets, play Horse and Pig, and then when it got dark, we'd go in his basement and play pool.

CINDEE: [*laughs*] Oh, my goodness.

HANK: So, we developed a fantastic friendship. We had some theological differences, but obviously were united on the essentials. He really modeled for me how you could disagree without being disagreeable. In other words, he modeled for me that we could disagree on some *major* doctrines — but still secondary doctrines — but that whole idea of "in essentials unity, in nonessentials liberty, and in all things charity" came home in a very practical sense through our relationship. So, early on as a brand-new Christian I was fortunate enough to become friends with R. C., and he had a tremendous impact on me. The big thing about R. C. is he certainly wasn't a perfect person but, I will tell you, he was the absolute real deal.

CINDEE: Yes.

HANK: *He was the absolute real deal.* I remember, not all that long before he died, he got permission to play golf, and he called me up — his nickname for me was Henry —

CINDEE: [*laughs*]

HANK: He called me up and said, "Henry, can you come to Orlando? We've got to play golf. The doctor's given me permission." So, we went out and played golf. He said, "You know, Vesta doesn't want me to play eighteen holes, but golf is not nine holes, it's eighteen holes." So, we played eighteen holes of golf. [*laughs*] We sat in the clubhouse afterward, had a couple beers, and talked. We had certain things we no longer discussed. He knew my view, and I knew his, and we just moved on beyond those things.

CINDEE: OK, now, I want to know, who's better at golf?

HANK: Well, I'll tell you, when we were first starting to play golf, in Ligonier, we were very evenly matched. This probably doesn't mean a lot to a nongolfer, but to a golfer, we were both four handicaps, at the time, when I first met him. He could flat play; that means you're a pretty good golfer for a handicap. So, he played great. I have memories of being better than him, but I'm sure he has memories of being better than me.

[*laughter*]

CINDEE: That's hilarious. You are so blessed — both of you to have that time together in the Lord and to have that fun time, too — that down time.

HANK: Yeah. I learned so much from him during those years. I used to listen to his tapes, used to ask him a lot of questions, but I learned a lot by example as well.

CINDEE: Yes. That's wonderful. Thank you for sharing all of that. How did you meet Walter Martin?

HANK: Well, we first met at Simon Greenleaf School of Law. I was doing a memory seminar there, and your dad was there sitting in the back row. He invited me to go to dinner with him, after I did the seminar, and then we started brainstorming. Your dad was just brilliant. He immediately started thinking, after hearing me, that we could take the cults and where they deviated from the historic Christian faith and use those deviations as springboards or opportunities for sharing the gospel. But, now, to make those memorable and to help people to be able to remember the information, not just hear it but remember it and thereby use the information as a way of reaching people. So, that's really how we first started our discussions and first began our friendship.

CINDEE: I was wondering if it might have been there. I was trying to strain my brain and remember as well where he said he'd first met you, and I could not remember.

HANK: Yeah, that's where we first met. I don't think we ever met before that; I think that was the first time.

CINDEE: What was the greatest thing you learned from Walter Martin?

The Bible Answer Man
Walter Martin and Hank Hanegraaff

HANK: Well, for many years we had a moniker, "Because truth matters"; and I think that if there is one thing that comes to mind immediately, he was a person willing to stand for truth — no matter the cost — doing what he did because *truth matters*. I remember him saying many times, "Tolerance when it comes to personal relationships is a virtue, but tolerance when it comes to truth is a travesty." So, he was a man committed to truth. *He lived for truth.* He knew that truth mattered, and that if you ever get to a place where civilization abdicates truth, you become not only post-truth but become post-Christian, and that's the milieu in which we find ourselves today.

CINDEE: Absolutely. What convinced you to accept his offer of becoming CRI's executive vice president? What motivated you to accept it?

HANK: Well, kind of an interesting situation if you look at it from an historical standpoint, because at the time, when Walter wanted me to come in and lead the ministry, my wife was *absolutely certain* that we would never move to California. So, when we were in discussions about this with the board, I decided to tell the board, and to tell your dad, that what I would do is I would do it from a distance — staying in Atlanta where we were living at the time — and commuting to Southern California. By the way, I never thought that your dad, or the board, would go along with it, but it was sort of my way of appeasing my wife and appeasing your dad. I said, "I'll commute." We decided to do that on a one-year trial basis. The board agreed and, most importantly, your dad agreed. So that's how I started working with CRI and leading CRI.

The reason I did it, from a personal standpoint, is I felt that I could offer a lot to CRI in terms of giving the ministry structure, accountability, and I felt that I had something significant to offer. The other side of the coin was very important to me. I had the opportunity to learn from your dad and to learn about apologetics, which I didn't know that much about. I knew a certain amount, but I wasn't a seasoned apologist. I certainly wasn't seasoned when it came to countercult ministry. So, I felt like it was a great opportunity to *add* to what I already learned through Evangelism Explosion. I knew how to share my faith, but I didn't know really, certainly not by the standard of your dad, how to take the objections to the Christian faith and use them as springboards or opportunities to share the gospel. So, I was learning a *tremendous* amount from your dad. I felt like, boy, this is a win/win situation — I have something to offer to CRI, and CRI has something that I can learn.

I had the incredible privilege of hanging out with the father of the countercult movement — I mean if you look at the whole countercult movement — your dad was *the father of that* and here I had the opportunity to hang out with him. So, it was fantastic. I felt like the year we were doing this, on a trial basis, you know, we'll see what happens at the end of the year. Well, in the middle of that year, your dad of course died of an occlusion of the right artery of his heart, and the rest is history again. Then it was no longer commuting. I immediately moved to Southern California and did what we had intended I would do if everything worked out after a year. Then, of course, there was no resistance from Kathy. "Yes, this is hand-to-plow move forward; this is God's calling on your life," she said.

CINDEE: Yes, absolutely. Well, I'm glad you had that time with him, Hank — to be mentored like that in those ways that you mentioned. I don't think you could have had a better mentor in terms of the cults, obviously, and apologetics. So, God definitely was positioning you there by teaching you — by my father teaching you — and grooming you to take that slot. Neither of you knew how bad the situation *really* was — how bad his health was. [Although I know that my father knew his days were short, I don't think even he recognized the Lord would take him as fast as he did.] I wondered where you were when you first heard my father was home with the Lord?

HANK: I can remember exactly where I was. It was a Monday morning. I was staying at a hotel. There was a Black Angus restaurant there, I can sort of see it all in my mind. I had come in to work with CRI.

CINDEE: OK.

HANK: I had just gone out for a walk in the morning, which was my habit. It was *very* early in the morning, and I got a call from Darlene, and the first words I heard were, "Hank, Walter's dead," and so, *that* [Hank sighs deeply] turned my world upside down.

CINDEE: Yes, indeed. [*sigh*] Well, it was wonderful of the Lord to work it out where you were in California at the time. I think that was definitely a blessing that you were right there.

HANK: Yes.

CINDEE: And Kathy was with you?

HANK: No, Kathy was not with me, but, of course, came immediately.

CINDEE: Moving away from that sadness — the earthquake that happened in California for you, for us, for CRI, and for everyone who loved my father and loved the ministry. It seemed like an earthquake, a pretty big one, had occurred on June 26, 1989. Moving past the grief and all that God got us through, I wondered, do you have any kind of a story, like an anecdote, during your friendship with my father — anything that stands out to you — any funny moment that you remember with him or an interesting exchange with him that stands out in your mind?

HANK: Well, your dad, he was just a one of a kind. So many things I remember about your dad. I remember being in a car with him, with my wife, and how he stopped at a little corner flower shop that he saw, and he bought my wife flowers. Just stopped the car and gave her flowers. Those kinds of things that he would do. I'd watch him eat, and he would say to me, "Hank, you know, all too many Christians are digging their own graves with their own knives and forks." And, then, he would be pouring Sweet & Low into his wine, mixing it, and drinking it. [*laughs*]

CINDEE: I remember that.

HANK: I would just laugh. And here's a story. I don't know if you want me to tell you this one, but I will.

CINDEE: OK.

HANK: I remember picking him up once. He had come to Atlanta to see me. I don't remember the exact circumstance. What I recall was that he was in the hotel — I went to pick him up at the hotel and knocked on the door. He opened the door, and he didn't have his toupee on.

CINDEE: Oh, OK. [*laughs*]

HANK: I just started laughing — not because he looked bad — it just was different, you know. I tried — I never told him the truth of why I was laughing, but it was just sort of a shock. It was sort of like when I had to cut off all of my hair — *it was a shock* — it was an accident where I was trimming my own hair, and I forgot to put the guard on, and I put a stripe right down the side of my head (back when I had hair), and I cut it all off.

HANK: You know my assistant Stephen. I did it at work, and I was trimming my hair — and Stephen's been with me forever — and I walked over to Stephen's desk and I said, "Stephen, look, will you do the honors?" And he finished the job.

The Bible Answer Man
Walter Martin and Hank Hanegraaff

CINDEE: [*laughs*] My goodness, so maybe down deep you just knew the *Bible Answer Man had* to be bald.

HANK: Exactly.

CINDEE: [*laughs*] That must have been it.

HANK: Yeah. I mean there are so many funny stories. There's one that you know — the one where your dad is doing a *Bible Answer Man* broadcast — he's leaning back in that old chair he had — and all of a sudden he leans too far, and he ends up on the floor while he's answering a question, and he never misses a breath or a beat, just as though nothing happened, lying flat on his back with his legs up in the air.

CINDEE: Oh, *yes*, I remember that. I think he was running late — he was always late.

HANK: I don't remember *all* the details. I just remember it taught me something. That no matter what happens, you *have* to have poise. [*laughs*] And he *definitely* had poise.

CINDEE: He did, he really did, and just you mentioning he answered the door without his toupee on — he really just was comfortable in his own skin.

HANK: Which is really cool; I never thought about it like that. Yeah, he could have not answered the door like that. He was just comfortable in his own skin.

CINDEE: He *really* was. He made fun of himself too, and he wasn't a prideful person. He would laugh at himself; he would laugh at others in a loving sort of way, and I really *loved* that about him. I wish I could have seen the look on your face when he opened the door, but I sort of can imagine. It doesn't surprise me that he did it because he was just that way.

HANK: Yeah.

CINDEE: You either loved him — people generally either loved him — or they didn't. What you see is what you get.

HANK: Well, the thing about it, and the reason I told you the story about the flowers, is because he had an unbelievably tender side.

CINDEE: Yes, he did. He really did. Thank you for sharing that, too; that's so sweet. Moving along here. What inspired you to write your first book?

HANK: When I became president of CRI, one of the *big* disappointments, I suppose for me, was not just the cults that were preying on the church, from without, but the corruption of the church from within.

CINDEE: Yes.

HANK: I was *terribly* bothered by the Word of Faith movement — by TBN at the time. The reason I was bothered by it is that I saw that, what in essence was happening, is that Christ was being reduced to a means to people's ends. Instead of being the end, he was just a means to their ends. People were invited to the Master's table not for love of the Master but rather for what was on the Master's table. So, it was a perversion of Christianity; it was turning Christianity on its head.

CINDEE: Yes.

HANK: I was very stirred up about all of that. So, in 1989, toward the end of the year — beginning of 1990 — I had in my mind that I wanted to write a book. I felt that God gave me the title: *Christianity in Crisis*. I really felt very strongly that I was called to do that, and I remember getting a lot of resistance first from Elliot Miller. One of the most endearing qualities about Elliot, for me, was that he was very forthcoming whenever he strongly disagreed with me; he did not have the same view of the Word of Faith movement that I did. He saw it more in line with the Charismatic/Pentecostal movement in general, as opposed to a perversion of Christianity. I remember having a tremendous amount of respect for Elliot, of course, for his position — for his longevity with CRI before I got there, for his relationship to your dad. So, I had a great respect for him.

I remember saying to Elliot, "Look. Let's talk this through, because I know you're a person of truth, and truth will win out. Either I'll agree with you and not write the book, or you'll agree with me and I'll write the book." As it turned out (in this particular case), he agreed with me. It was great because it established a friendship, a collegiality, and something that had enduring qualities for the ministry of the Christian Research Institute. He was one of those people, and there were many, that I would seek counsel from before I engaged in a project. This was a long project because the book wasn't published until 1993. So, I worked on that book for a *long* time. I was a new author, and when that book came out, it became a mega bestseller. Ironically, it not only had an impact in terms of selling a lot of copies but also spawned a lot of jealousy within the countercult community, because all of sudden here was this guy that really nobody knew about, and suddenly he was a best-selling author.

CINDEE: *Yes.*

HANK: It was interesting. I had a particular way in which I wanted to do that book. I formed that book around the acronym FLAWS. When the editor came — and I'm a perfectionist — I'd worked on the book for three years and he wanted to change the whole book. First, he wanted to change the title. Secondly, he said you can't use an acronym — that's too cutesy — you've got too much alliteration. I remember telling that editor, "You know what? This is my signature; this is how I write. I labored over every word; I'm not going to change it. If you don't want the book — if the publisher doesn't want the book — that's fine, but this is how I want to write the book." That, of course is the signature for all of my books and pretty much what all of my books have been forged around (acronyms), so that the material in the book becomes memorable for people, which is the very thing that started my relationship with your dad — to make things memorable.

CINDEE: Yes, absolutely, and you really hit a nerve. My father had that same concern about the prosperity gospel. He had been on TBN, of course, and had not been invited back. He had really confronted them. It was *really* a high priority of his to confront this.

HANK: You know, it's interesting you say that. For some reason or other, I probably knew that, but didn't understand how strongly your father felt until I started listening to some of his tapes.

CINDEE: Yes, and you really carried that torch. You really did because that was one of the highest things on his priority list that he was fighting at the time of his death.

HANK: Yes. That's right. That's absolutely true. Again, I went back and watched video. I listened to a message he had given. There's no question that what you are saying is true.

CINDEE: If you could be remembered for only one of your books (of the twenty-plus you've written), which book would you choose?

HANK: That's like asking me which one of my children I like best. That's a really difficult question to answer. I always say my best book is the one I'm working on. I'm working on a book right now titled *Truth Matters, Life Matters More: The Unexpected Beauty of an Authentic Christian Life*. That's the book that I am the most passionate about right now, that I am engrossed in writing. The book I think about often as a *very* significant book is a book titled *Has God Spoken?* The reason that book is so important to me is because it establishes the authenticity and authority of Scripture and does so in a memorable way. So, the first part of that book demonstrates the Bible is divine as opposed to merely human in origin, but the second part of that book is equally important because it teaches people to read the Bible in the way it's intended. In other words, people learn the art and science of biblical interpretation. It's an art in that the more you do it, the better you get at it. It's a science, in that rules apply.

One of the big problems is that you have people like Bart Ehrman, who has made a cottage industry out of discrediting the Bible. He will read a particular passage, and he'll read it not in the sense in which it's intended; so he gets something out of it that's not intended, concluding the Bible is inaccurate. So, he'll read, for example, a parable like the parable of the mustard seed. Jesus said the mustard seed is the smallest of all seeds, and orchid seeds are smaller, therefore Jesus has to be a false teacher; he tries to make a parable walk on all fours. We have the same problem in the Christian community as well. We have people who don't know how to read the Bible in the sense in which it's intended. As a result of that, they come with all kinds of fictitious paradigms that they impose on the Scriptures. Again, it gets back to the issue that you need to know how to read the Bible in the sense that it's intended.

CINDEE: I agree. One thing that I have admired about you for *so many years*, Hank, is your absolute unapologetic stand for the unborn. I have really been very proud of CRI for walking in the truth of God's Word in terms of the value of these unborn people that have their lives threatened and taken by abortion. You've supported me with my first book, *Rescue Me*, a pro-life time-travel thriller dealing with abortion, and have stood behind my pro-life songs as well: "Fearfully and Wonderfully Made" and "Who Will Save the Little Ones?" You have stood strong in your own efforts. *Whose Ethics? Whose Morals?* is the book that came out through you and CRI that deals with this matter as well. It's been such a joy to see you are a strong advocate for those who cannot speak for themselves. In your life, was there any kind of turning point when the pro-life issue hit you between the eyes and you were grieved by it, or have you always been pro-life?

HANK: Yes, I was always pro-life, but I'll tell you a couple of things. One is, I had early on in my Christian life become familiar with Francis Schaffer and was *very* impressed by a quote that I can't necessarily get perfect off the top of my head, where he said abortion would be the watershed issue of our generation. I think that was something that really impacted me — reading what Francis Schaffer said about abortion. I think on a practical level, on a personal level, I watched the birth of my children. It's the most beautiful thing you can possibly imagine, in my mind.

CINDEE: It is.

HANK: You see one human being come out of another human being, and you see the miracle of birth. You see the *miracle* of life, and you realize that baby was always a baby. That baby was in different stages of development, in the womb, but was always a child made in the image and likeness of God. To take the life of a child made in the image and likeness of God is *the ultimate abomination* because that child is so vulnerable.

CINDEE: Yes.

HANK: I think of my own wife. She was born prematurely. So, you see the horror of so many babies that have been aborted when they are five and a half months. Seeing the birth process on so many occasions with my wife had a visceral impact on me. I think this is one of the greatest holocausts in our midst — it's a holocaust that no longer has any excuse for it — in that we now have sonograms. There's no excuse whatsoever in thinking this is not a child. We know that this is a person from the moment of conception — not a fully developed personality but a person.

Now, of course, the abortion argument is shifting from people recognizing — because the sonogram says it — this is a human being, no question about it; but now they're saying there's a difference between acknowledging this is a human being and acknowledging one as having particular rights, meaning as that person develops, we decide when that person has rights. That's a *very* scary and slippery slope. There are now ethicists saying that the decision is not made while the child is in the womb but the decision can be made after the parents see the child and determine whether that child is worthy of life. So, you have Peter Singer of Princeton University and other ethicists saying it may be good to allow three days after the child is born. It's a very slippery slope, and I agree with Francis Schaffer. This is the watershed issue of our time.

CINDEE: Absolutely. What was your initial reaction to your cancer diagnosis?

HANK: Well, peace. I've been completely peaceful from the time I was diagnosed April 15, 2017, until the present. It's never changed. My sense was never that I was going to die — I don't mean that in a presumptive way, because I don't know. All the days ordained for me are written in his book before one of them came to be. So, I don't know how many years I have on this planet, but I never had a sense that I was going to die. I always had a sense that God was using this for purposes that are beyond my knowing. It has been one of the greatest experiences of my life. I can say that with all integrity. It's put me in touch with people that suffer. I've lived a charmed life from a health standpoint. I'd never been sick a day in my life; I don't even get colds. All of a sudden, I got a cough, in the early part of 2017, couldn't get rid of it, doctor told me this was just a bad virus going around; you just deal with it. Feeling something else was going on — I kept being persistent — I finally was sent to an oncologist, had a bone marrow biopsy, and realized that I had stage 4 mantle cell lymphoma. When I heard stage 4, I thought, well, it's terminal. So, immediately I started thinking I've got one more book to finish; will I have time to finish that book?

CINDEE: [*laughs*]

HANK: So, he was talking about chemotherapy right away. I started thinking — his voice was sort of like a distant voice in another room or something, because I wasn't really focused on him — I was trying to figure out how I was going to wrap up my life, quite frankly. When I came back to the present, and away from my internal thoughts, I said to the doctor — his name is Dr. Pal — "Well, what if I don't do the chemo? If it's stage 4, what's the point? Maybe I'd live as long, and I won't have to go through the chemo process and have all the poison pumped into my system."

He said, "Well, if you don't do chemo, you'll be dead in six months." I said, "Well, you know, I want to finish a book and be in good shape to finish the book and everything else."

And he said, "Hank, your particular cancer is mantle cell lymphoma, and stage 4 isn't terminal. You're thinking it's terminal, right?"

I said, "Yeah, it's what I thought when you said it's stage 4; that it's terminal."

He said, "No, no. It's not terminal. It's not *curable* right now — given the state of medicine — but it's not terminal. People go into long periods of remission." So, all of a sudden, I got a different perspective. When I heard stage 4, I thought, well, it's the end.

CINDEE: Yes.

HANK: It turns out it's one of the *worst* of the lymphomas, but it's also the lymphoma that they've had the best breakthroughs in.

CINDEE: Praise the Lord for that.

HANK: So, I went through a year of chemo, 2017, and the beauty of the chemo was it got the cancer out of my bones. I never went into full remission and the tumors came back this year, and so by God's grace I got into a clinical trial and the visible tumors — I think I showed it on Facebook — below my jaw.

CINDEE: You did.

HANK: That tumor just vaporized and disappeared in two and a half weeks. So, I'm assuming that the same thing is true internally. I'm having a PET scan in a week's time, so I'll know, for sure, but my blood markers are perfect. I mean, they're exactly the same as a healthy person. My hemoglobin is above fourteen, my white blood cell count is normal, my platelets, my potassium — I mean, every marker is perfect. The thing is, during the whole cancer period, it was fantastic because I saw how people really suffer. I think it's good to stare your own mortality in the face. It gives you a true valuation of things.

CINDEE: It does. Did you feel God nearer? Have you felt God nearer to you than any other time?

HANK: Well, yeah, a lot of reasons for that. I was Chrismated on April 9, Palm Sunday, and diagnosed April 15. Partaking of the real presence of Christ, I felt like I was sustained not just by biological energy but by an uncreated energy, for only God is uncreated. Quite frankly, my doctor — who's at the top of the food chain, when it comes to mantle cell lymphoma — whose name is Dr. Gosh, said he's never seen anybody go through stage 4 mantle cell lymphoma the way that I have. When I was having the chemo, I would go right back in and work.

CINDEE: I remember that. Amazing.

HANK: Yes, I did the show. I never missed a day of work except for when I was actually in the hospital. Every other chemo session was three days in the hospital. If I got out of the hospital by 3:00, I'd be in the studio by 6:00 doing the show. I 've continued doing my work completely unhampered by my disease. He says he's never seen anything like it. By and large, I don't have the appearance of having cancer. I feel great. I feel like I've had a supernatural experience — a miraculous experience with cancer.

CINDEE: Praise the Lord.

HANK: Now my prognosis looks *very* good. Likely, I'm in remission now. I met a doctor who was diagnosed, fifteen years ago, with mantle cell lymphoma, and he's still doing great.

CINDEE: Praise God.

HANK: He's in a maintenance program with an oral drug — which is all I'm taking right now, by the way, in the clinical trial. He's doing just fine. So, this cancer can go into remission for long periods of time — ten, fifteen, twenty years. Now they also have a new therapy called CAR T-cell, and it's an autoimmune kind of therapy. They take cells out of your body, reengineer them, reinsert them in your body, and it fights the cancer like heat-seeking missiles. It finds the cancer and kills it, and it's been very efficacious with other forms of cancer. It's not FDA approved for mine, yet, although I could do it if I wanted to because there are clinical trials I could get into. My doctor and I both feel — as well as other people that I've consulted — that I'm better off sticking with what I have right now. When this therapy is perfected — maybe five years down the line or whatever — then maybe use that as the next option.

[Follow Hank's ongoing heath updates at the *Bible Answer Man* Broadcast Facebook page.]

CINDEE: I have to ask you this question: a lot of Christians — when something terrible happens in their life — raise their fist at God and say *Why me?* It doesn't appear to me, from everything you've shared, you've ever had a *why me* moment but sounds like you have more of a testimony of *why not me?* I'm so moved by that. What do you think propelled you more toward the positive there? I think that the majority of Christians, when bad things happen, are not propelled toward the positive. What do you think pushed you in that direction so strongly?

HANK: Well, I'm living out what I've been teaching, which is to say, I have taught people on the *Bible Answer Man* broadcast, through my books, through my talks that God doesn't answer the *why* question. We have to learn to trust Him in the midst of our whys.

CINDEE: Yes.

HANK: So, I tell people, from Job, you know Job asks why, and God thunders back, "You don't even know how to create a tiny drop of dew. How would you understand what my purposes and what my plans are? Trust Me." I mean, that's the message. Trust Me. I've been teaching that for *many* years now, and I have the opportunity to live that out — to trust God in the midst of my whys. I've learned to trust Him. I've learned that God is trustworthy. So, I don't have to worry about what I can't understand. What I have to do is thank the Lord that He has demonstrated Himself to be trustworthy over and over again. It's the same thing with ministry — you have difficult times. We've had times of great deficits with our ministry financially. Well, if you look at the track record, you see that God has been faithful every single time. Right? And, you get to the next crisis, and you wonder is He going to be faithful this time. Then, the minute you wonder that, you think of the absurdity of that. There's a track record to go on.

CINDEE: That's right; and His track record is perfect.

HANK: Yes, and He moves you through different circumstances. He uses these circumstances to teach you things — to move you in different directions. In my case, I have a tremendous amount of empathy for people when I counsel them, whether it's on the *Bible Answer Man* broadcast or in other circumstances. There's a difference between having that empathy and actually *experiencing* suffering.

CINDEE: Yes.

HANK: So, it's a very good thing on many levels. So yes, I think the *why not me*, as you put it, is a really good way to put it.

CINDEE: Thank you for sharing all of that, Hank. How is your family doing with this whole process they have gone through with you? How are they holding up?

HANK: Well, fantastic. I think it's been *really* encouraging to them, and of course, you know, when you have a tight-knit family, as I do, it's fantastic. My daughter, Christina, came back from Hong Kong and she helped Kathy and the rest of the kids for a period of time. She helped me at the ministry. She came in and sort of held my hand while I was doing the *Bible Answer Man* broadcast, Facebook and all these kinds of things. Sometimes you're wondering, *Am I going to have the strength to get through it,* and she was there.

She's helped Kathy. You know cancer is a little bit of a full-time job added to a full-time job because you have to go for blood tests and this and that and the other thing. So, she was extremely helpful in keeping everything going, and she is still doing that, so I'm *very* grateful for the way my kids have rallied around me.

CINDEE: Yes. God's definitely given you a wonderful family, to say the least.

HANK: Yes.

CINDEE: Now moving in a different direction; something you had alluded to earlier was the discouragement you had with the Protestant Church. I want to ask you more specifically, what was troubling you, and what led you down the ancient path to Greek Orthodoxy?

HANK: I did get very discouraged with all the winds and waves of doctrines that are sweeping through the church, particularly today. Things like — all of a sudden — it becomes a fad not to confess your sins. Now, all of a sudden, you have Christian teachers — not just fringe teachers but very-well-known apologetic titans — teaching that you can't confess your sins; you really can't use the Lord's Prayer because that's Old Covenant. God's forgiven you, so if you ask for forgiveness again, or if you confess your sins, it's like spitting in the face of God. And this gets traction, and it's lauded. Or, going back a few years, you have *The Prayer of Jabez*. Also, if you learn a particular formula, a capricious God will answer your prayers, but you have to know the formula — and then you get the parts out of heaven and answers to your prayers. All these winds and waves of doctrine are sweeping through the church to a large degree because of the fissuring that's taking place within Protestantism — meaning that every single year there are so many hundreds, if not thousands of people, who have the gift of speaking — or charisma — and they hang up a shingle and start a new permutation. They have a particular angle, and that becomes a new movement, and that becomes a new book. Quite frankly, after a while, I got discouraged with it and I thought, you know, I wonder how church was originally done. Is there any way of knowing that? Because, really, quite frankly, you can be biblically literate but very historically illiterate.

CINDEE: That's right.

HANK: And, so, you wonder, is there any record of how the church was done? Can you go back to Ignatius of Antioch and get any information from him on how church was done at the time of the transition from the apostles to the early apologists and early fathers of the church? Is there anything that we can learn? So, I started digging into this. This is sort of my habit. When I wrote my book *The Apocalypse Code* on eschatology, I didn't write it until I'd been doing the *Bible Answer Man* broadcast for fifteen years. So, when people would ask me questions about eschatology, I would say, "Well, here are the various views; I'm not qualified." I need to memorize the Book of Revelation. So, I didn't feel like I was qualified to speak on the topic. So, I'd give the various views but eventually I felt I was qualified, and I wrote the book *The Apocalypse Code*.

CINDEE: Rick loves that book, by the way. He's read it two or three times.

HANK: I'm glad. You know it's my son David's favorite book as well. So, the same thing happened with me looking into church history, and saying, wow, you can look at the Didache for example and see this is how they did church. So, as I looked historically, I found that you look at the ancient church; it never tried to be innovative. It tried to perpetuate the Judeo-Christian tradition from Judaism through the time of Christ, through the time of the apostles, to the followers of the apostles, to the apologists, and to the early church fathers. What I liked about the early church was it was trying to perpetuate; it was not trying to innovate. They hammered out the great creeds through the great ecumenical counsels. They hammered out *very* important things with respect to the nature of God. I fell in love, really, with the church fathers. You think of the Arian/Athanasian dispute and Athanasius saying *Athanasius contra mundum*: Athanasius against the world — here I stand. And, you see the early church fathers who stood for these *great* doctrines with respect to the nature of God.

CINDEE: Yes.

HANK: The fact that Christ was, in fact, divine. That He wasn't a mere creature. The fact that He's one person with two natures, 100 percent human and 100 percent divine. All this was hammered out in the ecumenical councils and creeds as a legacy for the body of Christ. The early Nicene Council in 325 through the later Nicene Council in 787 where you have the big iconoclastic controversy, where people were destroying icons, and then you have the church say *no*. The church unanimously said no. If you destroy icons, you have a bad Christology because Christ is an icon; He's the icon of God! You have a diminished view of the Incarnation. For Christ came and appeared. The church determined that, no, these are *windows* into the spiritual world. You can't *worship* icons, but you can *venerate* them. They are the heroes of the faith that are depicted in the great faith hall of fame in Hebrews chapter 11, et cetera.

CINDEE: Right. When you say venerate, you're saying esteem. You highly esteem them.

HANK: Exactly. Like Mary. You think about how she was highly esteemed. She was chosen out of all the people on the planet, you know, to undo what Eve did. Eve was deceived. The first woman Eve was deceived. The second woman, Mary, conceived and bore *God* — *Theotokos*, the God-bearer. So, you venerate Mary — you never worship her — but you venerate her because she is *chosen*, highly esteemed of God, to bring God into the world. It's a wonderful thing. You can never say that Christianity is patriarchal, because the icon of greatest value to a Christian, the greatest exemplar, is a woman — Mary — a woman of *humility* chosen to be the vessel to bring God into the world. It's just incredible. It gives me goosebumps even as I'm speaking about it, quite frankly. The idea is that you have a history. So, to get back to what I was saying earlier, instead of all of these winds and waves of doctrine, you can go back to what was *hammered out* in the church councils in the creeds — you think of the Nicene creed, for example, uniformly accepted by all Christians.

CINDEE: Right.

HANK: These creeds and these councils have *incredible* import. There's a sense of liberation that I have with all of it too, because I can go back and not feel I have to innovate in the twenty-first century, but I can go back and say, what did the church fathers say? We're Pygmies standing on the shoulders of giants. So, I don't think I need to feel as though somehow or other I have some new revelation in the twenty-first century like the Catholics do or many of the Protestants do. The Pope can speak *ex-cathedra* and now all of a sudden you have limbo and purgatory and you have the immaculate conception of Mary, and have all these kinds of innovative doctrines.

CINDEE: That they're adding.

HANK: That they're adding. And, the ancient church, they'll never do that. They'll never change. They'll never innovate.

CINDEE: And, what you've really done is gone to the source. My father used to always say to go to the *primary* source. You've peeled back the layers of centuries, and you've tried to understand, from the beginning, what was the church? I think it's absolutely critical more Christians do that.

HANK: I think it's important to say in this context, I'm not suggesting to anyone that the Orthodox Church is a panacea; it's not. It's a great mission field, quite frankly. There's a truism — that *tradition* is the living faith of the dead, but *traditionalism* is the dead faith of the living. Traditionalism unfortunately has impacted the Orthodox Church all over the world. Quite frankly, if you talk to the Patriarchs, the Archbishops, or the Metropolitans — talk to the leadership of the Orthodox Church — they understand their own dilemma. So, it's a great mission field. In no way am I suggesting that this is the only way to go. What I am saying, though, is it has committed me more than ever to mere Christianity, as C. S. Lewis put it, or as we have always said at Christian Research Institute (this goes back to the time of your dad): in essentials, unity; in nonessentials, liberty; and in all things, charity. God has His people everywhere. He's got His people all over the place.

CINDEE: He does.

HANK: The real thing we have to be is galvanized around the essentials of the Christian faith.

CINDEE: That's right.

HANK: That's what I stand for as president of the Christian Research Institute.

CINDEE: That's right, absolutely, and you saying there's a mission field inside the Greek Orthodox Church. I look at it as there being a mission field in the Greek Orthodox Church, the Catholic Church, and the Protestant Church. There's a wide mission field running through it all because, as Scripture says, the wheat grows with the tares.

HANK: That's well said.

CINDEE: And, I really think the way you've explained all of this, too, is *tremendously* helpful. Do you have a difference of opinion of American Orthodoxy versus cultural Orthodoxy in Europe?

HANK: Well, there are no real differences, honestly. I sometimes joke that the only difference are the pastries that you find in the fellowship hall, you know, whether you're talking about a Slavic church or an Antiochian church or a Greek Orthodox church or a Russian Orthodox church. The liturgy is pretty much the same. Unfortunately, there's a cultural dimension that oftentimes overrides the true faith, where this just becomes a habit as opposed to a living reality.

The thing that probably I love the most — in terms of communicating the essence of Orthodoxy — is a quote by Vladimir Lossky. I probably won't get this word-for-word, but what he said was following the fall, the history of humanity is a history of shipwreck awaiting rescue. And then he said, but the port of salvation is not the goal; the goal is for the shipwrecked to continue on a journey whose sole goal is union with God. What that in essence is communicating is the difference between *transactionalism* and *transformation*, meaning that so much of the Christian world is about transaction. So, I pray a prayer. Now I get this card that keeps me out of hell — gets me into heaven — and I keep living like a baptized secular humanist.

CINDEE: Right. It's like a name-it-and-claim-it salvation pass.

HANK: Yes. It's just a transaction I had with God. And, now I say, well, you know, I had this transaction, so I'm set. Well, what Vladimir Lossky is saying is, Look, the port of salvation is not the goal; it's not that it's unimportant. If you're shipwrecked, and you're saved from the water, I mean you're *very* happy. Well, if you're shipwrecked and you got saved from the water, you don't want to get saved just to that rescue station — the port of salvation; you want to continue on the journey of life. You got rescued from the waves, and now you want to continue. And, what is that goal? The sole goal is union with God, which is to say the goal is to have fellowship in the Trinity — that we have been brought into the inner sanctum to have fellowship with the Father, Son, and Holy Spirit. That's the essence that I really appreciate in Orthodoxy — that emphasis. It's not a journey that you go alone; you have to do it in the spiritual gymnasium, which is the church, where you can receive by grace what God is by nature. You don't become a god by nature, you become, as Peter put it, "a partaker of the divine nature." I think that is something that is lost in most of Evangelicalism — too transactional; it's not transformational. Now, of course, again as I said, you can have Orthodox people who are just going through the rituals not realizing that this is supposed to be transformational.

CINDEE: Right, as is true in the Protestant Church, as well, in a lot of cases. So, I love that quote you mentioned, and I think that it's important that people understand that there *has* to be transformation. The goal is to *know* God and to be God-like — not be God — but to *know* Him as your Savior. I don't know how many times I've heard people say so-and-so got saved in camp, and I know they're with the Lord (even though there was absolutely no fruit in their lives). That's been my experience in the Protestant Church at times. I've heard those testimonies — grieving parents or people who are grieving for their friends — "Well, they accepted Christ back then." What people need to understand is that salvation, and coming to Jesus Christ, produces *change*. So, while we're not saved by our works, our works are evidence that we are truly saved. The fruit of our lives *is* the evidence. I think people are losing that in a lot of directions, and it's spiritually dangerous for many.

HANK: Yes. Exactly what you say is right, and you look at what James says about all of this: show me your faith without your deeds, and I'll show you my faith by what I do [James 2:18].

CINDEE: That's right.

HANK: And, even the rhetorical foolish man — do you want evidence that faith without deeds is useless? Was not our ancestor, Abraham, considered righteous for what *he* did when he offered his son Isaac on the altar? You see that his faith and his actions were working together, and his faith was made complete by what he did.

CINDEE: Yes.

HANK: James later on says that you see a person is justified by what he does and not by faith alone. Now, the Orthodox take that passage and they don't say, well, Ephesians 2:8, 9 is now negated. No, they say you are saved by God's grace through faith. They *affirm* you cannot save yourself by what you do. But, what they *don't* do (which happens in sort of the Western church in general) is they don't try to put faith in opposition to works, as though the two are competing. As you well said it a moment ago, your faith is validated by what you do. And so, there are many examples in James, and you have the example of Abraham. You also have the example of Rahab the prostitute — considered righteous for what she did when she gave lodging to the spies and then sent them off in a different direction. So, James concludes that the body without the spirit is dead; faith without deeds is dead.

CINDEE: Amen.

HANK: It's never "You have to juxtaposition one against the other." It just doesn't happen in the Eastern Church. That's another thing I love about the Eastern Church. They don't try to explain mysteries. You can't explain how

Christ can be one person with two natures. It's beyond our understanding. And, how Christ can really be present in the Eucharist. There are things that we just leave in the realm of mystery. It's beyond our ability to fully comprehend, but we trust God's Word.

CINDEE: Yes, because we see through a glass darkly, as Scripture says. Just your bringing up the Eucharist makes me think of Martin Luther. I've been reading more about him in recent months. He, of course, believed in Christ's presence in the Eucharist, as you have come to believe yourself. What are your thoughts about Martin Luther? He was actually very Catholic at the time of his death. He wanted reform in the Catholic Church — regarding things that troubled him — but he didn't want to leave it.

HANK: Well, he was a very complex controversial person. That's a big subject, but let me say that what you just described is absolutely accurate. In fact, it's interesting that twelve years after the inaugural event of the Reformation, in 1529, there was a great debate between Luther and Zwingli, the Swiss Reformer, at the Marburg Castle, and already the Reformation starting fissuring; it started fracturing. So, there are *many* splits within the Reformation twelve years after Martin Luther nailed the theses on the Catholic door in Wittenberg. So, there was this debate between Zwingli and Luther. Zwingli was accusing Luther of bread worship. He was saying, how can you believe that Christ is really present? It's a memorial; it's a remembrance. How can you say Christ is really present? Luther's response was very measured. He said if he could disagree with the papists on this, he would, but he can't. This is the understanding of the church throughout all of history. I can't go against all that. And he said to Zwingli, as part of his response, well, if you can explain to me how Christ can be one person with two natures, I'll explain to you how Christ can really be present in the Eucharist. So, he left it in the realm of mystery.

CINDEE: Yes.

HANK: Again, he said, if he could disagree with the papists on this, he would, but he can't disagree with what was, at the time, 1500 years of church history.

CINDEE: Right. Exactly. I struggle with the fact that you have had a lot of attack on you since you joined the Greek Orthodox Church. I struggle personally with these affronts because I look at Martin Luther and have been studying some of the church fathers. I look at all of this and I think that if people would just understand — would do some homework — they could understand your path much more clearly. Martin Luther was *really* Catholic.

You're not Catholic; you're Greek Orthodox, which is distinctively different, and yet I feel like you have had a rough ride since you were Chrismated and since you joined the Greek Orthodox Church. I think if people had a better understanding of who Martin Luther really was, they could see that you are truly a brother, as he was. You are a brother in Christ as well. Just because your path has been to look back to the ancient church and find your way to see where everything connects, that does not make you come out not as a believer — it is a believer looking at the roots of the ancient church, which I think is very honorable, actually. I see people quoting Martin Luther on Facebook, of course, and all over the place. I think to myself, how can they be so reverent of him, an icon in a real sense, and yet some people have kind of categorized you differently than Martin Luther — *in a disparaging way* — which really doesn't logically make sense if you know the facts of history. What do you say to people that say, "No; he has left the faith"? That's such a harsh judgment and certainly is false.

HANK: Well, I sympathize with people who have that response because *very* few people know what Greek Orthodoxy is all about. You've alluded to this. People think it's a form of Catholicism (it's not), nor was there ever a Reformation in the Eastern Church. The Eastern Church had its own struggles. There's a split between the Eastern Orthodox and the Eastern Oriental Orthodox Church, which is not completely resolved to this day. So, they had their own issues, but Eastern Orthodoxy is not Western Christianity. Rome and the Reformers had more in common as quarreling cousins than Orthodoxy has in common with Roman Catholicism. I think people (I don't want to be harsh) are biblically illiterate and, in some cases, are historically illiterate as well. The spit between the Eastern and the Western church took place in 1054. The Western church had a completely different experience than the Eastern Church had. So, if you're a Western Christian, you don't know what's going on in the Eastern Church, and, quite frankly, I knew that the Eastern Church was the Church of the Seven Ecumenical Councils. I never spoke disparagingly about the Eastern Church, but until I got into it myself, I never understood Orthodoxy all that well. There was a learning curve for me, and I can understand how people look at this and they — you have the trolls on the web — they'll say *Hank Hanegraaff has left the Christian faith*. They don't know what to think. So, I sympathize with that. You know, unfortunately, we live in an era of time where people want to think the worst and they want to say sensationalistic things, but I think that people who have known me for many years know I don't go off half-cocked.

CINDEE: No.

The Bible Answer Man
Walter Martin and Hank Hanegraaff

HANK: Meaning that my goal is simply not to do what is expedient, what is popular, what is politically correct. I learned that from your dad. "The pulpit is not the place for a popularity contest," your dad used to say.

CINDEE: That's right.

HANK: This is not for me a popularity contest. I learned at the end of the day, I'm not going to answer to an internet troll. I'm not trying to disparage anybody. I'm simply saying that's not who I am going to answer to. Who I will answer to is God.

CINDEE: Yes.

HANK: And, I will stand before Him and give an answer — an account of my life. So people can say whatever they want about me, you know. I'm acutely aware of my own imperfections, but the person I'm concerned about is the Triadic One. I'm concerned about the Father, Son, and the Holy Spirit, concerning me.

CINDEE: Yes, absolutely.

HANK: Will our Lord say, "Well done, good and faithful servant," or will my work be tested as being wood, hay, and stubble as opposed to gold, silver, and precious stones? It's really immaterial to me what people say except how it affects other people in either building them up spiritually or breaking them down.

CINDEE: Yes.

HANK: I think that there are unfortunately all kinds of people who don't have discernment. They read the hysteria — the internet lies, or whatever you call it these days, fake news. Whatever. [*laughs incredulously*] You can't do anything about it; it's the world we live in, but what you have to do is walk uprightly before God and other people, and let the chips fall where they may. In saying all of that, I sometimes think when people say things that are untrue about me, I think, well, if they could see me as God sees me, they would know that I'm a sinner saved by grace. Meaning, I'm not guilty of the things they accuse me of, but I'm a sinner guilty before God.

CINDEE: Yes, as we all are. You know, I've told you this before, when you first joined the Greek Orthodox Church, I didn't know anything about it. I was one of those people — I felt like there was a theological cardiac arrest in the Evangelical world. [*laughs*] And I was part of that in my lack of ability to understand the direction this was that you are in. I did listen to people online, some, I prayed about that, and it really wasn't until I did my own investigation — really followed church history — and got to the sources in order to understand where you were coming from and what your path was. It was when I did that with Rick that we really began to understand clearly that you had made a choice that may not be what every Christian makes (a church choice), but it certainly wasn't a choice that took you away from Jesus Christ. In fact, the Lord has used your choice to draw you closer to Him.

HANK: Absolutely.

CINDEE: And, so, I feel like I understand in some sense some of the misunderstandings out there because I know I was that person at that time too wondering, OK, what is that Church? What do they believe, and is that OK? I was *so* uninformed. I think this has been such a great thing because it's caused me to really look back through history, really be blessed, and enjoy marking the path of church history to where we are today. It's been an interesting journey. Until people are willing to actually see the path backward that brought us to where we are today, they can't begin to grasp that what you are doing is not apart from Christianity. You are under the Christian umbrella, and like you *always* say, "In essentials, unity," and that's where our focus needs to be. There are too many things around us we need to be looking out for. This certainly is not one of them.

HANK: Well, I appreciate you saying that. It's very, very helpful.

CINDEE: I think that your journey has helped us open up our minds and hearts in a direction I had never been before in my understanding. We know you as a brother, and love you as a brother, and we wanted to understand. I think that's what we're supposed to do with each other. We're supposed to *try* to understand. We're supposed to seek one another out. We came to you, and you were loving; you gave us answers. That was a good example of how we are supposed to treat one another, in love, in these kinds of circumstances. I just really applaud you for that.

HANK: Thank you, Cindee. That means the world to me.

CINDEE: Changing directions once again, I want to ask you about Elliot Miller — our mutual dear friend and brother — who had his own battle with cancer and is now with the Lord. Can you share a couple of thoughts about Elliot and maybe some of your last moments together? I'd heard from

Corinne that you had brought them groceries and that they were so blessed by your visits to them during the time that Elliot was getting close to going home to be with the Lord.

HANK: Well, I alluded to this earlier, Elliot — like your dad — was committed to truth, and when he was dying, I remember him asking me questions about how I was able to write so many books and he was saying to me, "Sometimes I feel like I haven't done enough." I said, "Elliot, you cast such a large shadow. You've been so faithful for so many years." And, he started weeping. He said, "I'm going to take that with me to my grave." He was truly a person who cast a long shadow, I mean, he was a person who was known for truth. I'll tell you the greatest story from my perspective is what he did with what's known as the Lord's Recovery, or the Local Churches. He was at the fountainhead of writing materials that castrated this group as being cultic. My friend, Sealy Yates, suggested that I meet with The Recovery; they wanted to meet with me. He felt like it was a worthwhile thing to do.

CINDEE: Yes.

HANK: You know, meet and talk, and so I did. The things that we believed about them, they said, "No, we're not modalists — we're thoroughly Trinitarian — we don't believe that we can be like God is in the godhead. We don't believe that we're the only church," et cetera. Elliot and Gretchen Passantino (who was also a titan in the apologetic world, what a great person she was), they had been at the fountainhead of writing information about this group. When I met with them, I felt like a neophyte, I don't really know much about this group. I know a little bit; I know about our statements, and so forth. I wasn't really at the fountainhead as Gretchen and Elliot were. So, I decided to bring them into this project because I felt that they would look at this from the standpoint of CRI — the position that CRI had always held, but also because I knew they were both people of truth.

CINDEE: Yes.

HANK: And, of course, Elliot and Gretchen were just *deeply* committed to truth. They had such an incredible impact in mentoring me over the years. I'll be eternally grateful to both of them. Anyway, I figured if anyone could get to the bottom of this, it would be Elliot Miller. He had every motivation, I would say, to affirm his earlier position, which was the position of CRI. I assigned him and Gretchen to this project, and Elliot did first-rate primary research on this project. Elliot wasn't the quickest person in the world, but he was thorough — that's why he wasn't quick.

CINDEE: Yes.

HANK: The project lasted six years and ended up with a special issue of the CHRISTIAN RESEARCH JOURNAL: "We Were Wrong." That JOURNAL has transformed the lives of so many people around the world. I hear stories, when I travel around the world, of families, who were broken and separated because of this issue, reunited. Just…transformational stories. This was a function of Elliot saying, well, I don't want to have egg on my face, but I'm willing to follow truth wherever it leads. I think this is one of the great characteristics of Elliot Miller that I appreciated about him. I appreciate many things about him. He was *very* funny. When he laughed, you could hear it throughout the whole ministry. He would just laugh. I went to visit him in the hospital one time when he had diverticulitis, I believe it was. He was dealing with a perforation and was in a lot of pain and everything else. So, he was in a hospital bed, and Corinne was there. I walked in and the nurse was there with Elliot. Elliot perked up and said, "*That's my boss.*" I could tell he was in pain and so I tried to bring a little levity to the circumstance. I said, "Elliot, you know, I've got to get something off my chest. Something really bothers me about you — in fact, a couple of things that really bother me. Everything that I do, you copy me."

CINDEE: [*laughs*]

HANK: And, he's looking at me real intently, and Corinne doesn't know what's going to happen. First of all, we have the same birthday.

CINDEE: Yes.

HANK: So, I say, "I'm born July 18, and you have to copy me. I get stage 4 cancer, and you have to copy me *again*." And, Elliot, when he laughs, it's like hair-on-fire laughing. [*laughs*]

CINDEE: I know. [*laughs*]

HANK: He burst out laughing because all of a sudden he realized I was just playing with him, which I used to do all the time. He said, "Well, Hank, I can't let you have all the glory." [*laughs*] He was a great guy.

CINDEE: Yes.

HANK: He wasn't cookie cutter. He was just a unique human being.

CINDEE: He certainly was, and he lives on with our Lord. He's out of the battle now.

HANK: Well, there's no question about that. He suffered — it was difficult to see him. In fact, I told Stephen and Paul Young (of course, they've been here for almost thirty years each), I told them I came back from my last visit with Elliot, and I told them if you want to see Elliot before he dies, you need to go right now. I said, I don't think he's going to be with us much longer. I could just tell; he had that look. He had that death rattle. So, I didn't think he would survive his cancer, and fortunately I was able to spend real good quality time with him before he died.

CINDEE: I'm glad for that. We did have some phone time. I wish we could have seen him again, but we're thankful for the time we had, and definitely (even just talking to him on the phone) we could tell also, and you had filled us in, it was very evident it was his time. God was calling him.

HANK: Yes. Absolutely.

CINDEE: Switching gears again on you, what do you perceive is the greatest modern-day threat to the church?

HANK: Well that's an interesting question. There are a number of ways I would answer that. On the one hand, if you think about threats from without, I look at the forces of insistent secularism — philosophical naturalism, scientism — the -isms of our day. They're the new cults of our day. So, you have the forces of insistent secularism on the one hand, and then you have Islamic jihad on the other. Islam is growing; it's the fastest-growing religion in the world. It is filling a vacuum that is left by native populations in the Western world dying out. If you look at Western civilization, in general, it's not just related to Europe; you can talk about New Zealand and places like that, people who have been affected by the Christian ethic that built their economies. Those native populations are dying out. Simple demographics — the birthrate is far less than the death rate and so the native populations are dying out. Filling the vacuum are millions of polygamist Muslims who have no intention whatsoever of assimilating into Western culture.

CINDEE: True.

HANK: And, so, that's the proverbial python swallowing its prey with a long and slow digestion. Let me say that having said that those are both great threats against the Christian church, the *greatest* modern-day threat to the church today is not external; it's internal. Pagans are always going to exercise their job description. So, the question becomes, *Are Christians are going to exercise their job description?* And the problem is that the answer is roundly, no. The church is lethargic. The church has lost its way in the West. So, pagans do what pagans naturally do. The question is, will Christians do what they were commissioned to do? We're ambassadors for Christ. Most Christians are secret agents. I usually joke they haven't blown their cover before the unregenerate world. And Jesus said it very plainly. If the salt loses its saltiness, how will it be made salty again? It's no longer good for anything except to be thrown out and trampled by men. This is essentially what we've found. We have an impotent church.

CINDEE: I think so, too.

HANK: A church that is a microcosm of the world. You think about if you took a pound of salt and put it in a quart of water, that water would be *very* salty. You look at the number of professing Christians — or the people who take the name of Christ upon their lips in our culture — you would think that our culture would be pretty salty, that the Christian ethic would permeate the culture. We'd be transformational agents in the culture, but that's not happening. So, the only thing you can assume is that the salt is in Ziplock bags in the water and is not permeating the water at all. Not only that but many Ziplock bags, so that the salt is separated from each other because there's so much division within the church. So, I think the biggest threat against the church is its own apathy. So the church has to again regain a vision for making disciples — this is the Great Commission, which has become the great omission of the church. The power of deification, as Peter said, becoming partakers of the divine nature; that is what should animate the church. That's what gives us a power that is in us but not of us. Paul talks about this when he says in Colossians, "We proclaim Christ, admonishing and teaching everyone with all wisdom so that everyone may be perfected in Christ." Then he says, "To this end I am energized by all of His energy which so powerfully energizes me" (see Colossians 1:28–29). This means that we can work on our own power, we can be on the sidelines not working at all, or we can operate with all of His energy.

CINDEE: Yes, His power.

HANK: So, we have to be energized by power that is in us but not of us. The ingrafted life — not just changed life but the exchanged life — the life of Christ within. That well that Jesus Christ talked about to the woman at the well. That is living streams of water from within, so you thirst no more. So, you need discipleship, but it has to be powered by a power in us but not of us, as I just said. And, I think we have to use the means that God has given us. We have to use the digital highways, the digital platforms that God has given. The means of interconnectivity for the first-century church were the Roman roads. The interconnectivity for the modern church is the digital highway. It's important that we utilize that but utilize it properly — never replace the embodied church life.

CINDEE: No.

HANK: The last thing I'll say, in this regard, is I think it's critical that the church recognizes this unity in essentials. Benjamin Franklin said, "If we don't hang together, we're going to hang separately." I think we need to work together on common-cause issues. That the fissuring in the church has to become fusion. Fusion is hard; it takes a lot of work.

CINDEE: Yes, this was C. S. Lewis's point from *Mere Christianity*, too, trying to draw people together on the essentials. And to love one another.

HANK: Yes, isn't this what the Lord said? He said, "I do not pray for these alone, but also for those who will believe in Me through their word; that they all may be one, as You, Father, are in Me, and I in You; that they also may be one in Us, that the world might believe that You sent Me" (John 17:20–21 NKJV).

CINDEE: Amen.

HANK: Now, that's the Lord praying, and we can't say that's impractical and it's not going to happen. Look, we can't say that. If the Lord prayed this, we have to *move* in that direction as well. This is not a Kumbaya unity at all costs; it is a unity around the essentials of the Christian faith. Within that context, we can work together. We not only can but we must. If we don't, we're going to be impotent in the face of what I just mentioned — the two great threats: the forces of insistent secularism on the one hand and Islam jihad on the other.

CINDEE: Yes, absolutely. It's interesting, too, as you were talking, I was thinking back to an interview I saw of my father. It was on TBN, in the 1980's, and one of the burdens of his heart was how dark the Evangelical church had grown. And how the Protestant movement and all people were really going astray. His concern was your concern. Open up those bags and pour out the salt. Where's the salt? Where's the light? Wake up, church.

HANK: Yes, that's right.

CINDEE: He had the same clarion call.

HANK: He was prophetic. He was prescient.

CINDEE: You both were in sync with so much. I can really see the hand of God having had both of you there then, and you now. When you arrive in heaven someday (God willing, decades from now), who besides Jesus Christ do you want to fellowship with first and why?

HANK: That's a hard question to answer because when we get to heaven, we're going to see things from a different perspective than the way we see them here. Meaning that the heroes we have here pale by comparison to the heroes we see there. There are so many heroes. We think of the heroes who have the platforms — the big-name Evangelicals who have gone on before us — the big names within the early church. I mentioned some of them. We think of them immediately, right? The Martin Luthers — these are the things that come to mind. My sense is that when we get there, we're going to find some person that maybe we didn't respect, or think much of, because they didn't meet the standards that we set in our own minds. It's like the woman that gives the mite, right, and Jesus sees that woman and commends that woman because she's given out of her poverty. I think we will have a completely different valuation of things than we do right now. I temper my remarks by that qualification. Obviously, the people that were heroes to me, your dad included — I mean, these are people you want to have conversations with…my dad who has gone on into eternity. The reunion with people that we've talked about during this *podcast* I would call it — this has turned into a podcast! [*laughs*] But, you know, the Gretchen and Bob Passantinos, Elliot Miller, my good friend R. C. Sproul, and so *many* others, even people that I've had some disagreements with. Those disagreements will have vanished when we get into eternity because now we're going to see things as they really are, and we're going to be able to love as we are loved, in a true sense, not *phileo* love necessarily by itself or *eros* love but *agape* love. We're going to have God's love, and so I think we'll see things differently, but obviously, the people that I mentioned — and many others — are people we will enjoy a reunion with. I think about our baby Grace that died as a preborn child. I think about the idea of rushing into her arms in eternity.

CINDEE: Yes.

HANK: Yes, it's beyond our capacity to understand the joy that we'll experience at that time.

CINDEE: That's right. Very well said. What godly counsel would you give to your children and your grandchildren if they someday hear (read) this — and you're home with the Lord — and they're listening to Grandad — or Grandpa? What do you go by? Are you called Grandad or Grandpa?

HANK: Boy, all kinds of names.

CINDEE: You're called all kinds of names? [*laughs*]

HANK: Papa, sometimes Grandpa. [*laughs*] The kids have their own little standards, but it's all wonderful.

CINDEE: What godly counsel — you're speaking right to them now — if they ever tune in and hear you talking, what do you want to say to them?

HANK: Well, you know the first thing that comes to mind, Cindee, is, "Only one life, twill soon be past, only what's done for Christ will last."

CINDEE: Amen.

HANK: That's the thing I think about all the time. That's what Paul says in 1 Corinthians 3. There's only one foundation, and that foundation is Jesus Christ. On that foundation, you can build using wood, hay, and straw, or you can build using precious materials — the gold, the silver, the precious stones. The Lord will reveal that day what you built with. If you built with inferior materials, the image that Paul gives us is that you'll be saved but only as someone escaping through the flames. So, it's the idea of a man rushing out of a burning building with nothing but charred clothes upon his back. You'll be saved, but you'll have no reward. What did Jesus talk about all the time? He talked about reward. "Behold I come quickly, and my reward is with Me to give to everyone according to what he has done. Do not labor for that which is perishing, but labor for that which is eternal." Jesus said, "Don't lay up for yourselves treasure where moth and rust corrupt or thieves break in and steal but lay up for yourselves treasures in heaven where moth and rust can't corrupt, or thieves can't steal. For where your treasure is, there your heart will be also" (see Matthew 6:19–21).

The Bible Answer Man
Walter Martin and Hank Hanegraaff

CINDEE: Amen.

HANK: So, if your treasure is in heaven, that's where your heart is. If your treasure is on Earth, that's where your heart is, too. It is difficult because, by all standards, we live in a *very* wealthy country. I've traveled around the world, and the poorest among us are relatively wealthy. The great thing is not wealth but storing up for yourself treasures in heaven.

CINDEE: Yes.

HANK: And, wealth is *so* easy to become addicted to. Jesus said it's easier for a poor man to enter heaven than for a rich man. The riches have a way of intoxicating us. This is why sometimes it's good to have some falls — to have some economic falls even when we were going through the Great Recession. It's kind of good. It gives you a little semblance of what people are going through around the world on a regular basis. I'd want them to know that the big thing is to lay up for yourselves treasures in heaven. I'm firmly convinced that there are degrees of rewards in heaven and degrees of punishments in hell. What we do now counts for all eternity.

CINDEE: Yes, that's Scriptural. What is your life's verse?

HANK: Well, I've had various life verses through the years, but you know the one that I sign all of my letters with now — and I have been for a long time — because at the Christian Research Institute, we now say it's not only "because truth matters"; it's that "*life and truth matter.*" That really comes from 1 Timothy 4:16. "Watch your life and doctrine closely." The doctrine I would equate to truth. "Persevere in them because if you do, you will save both yourself and your hearers." So, the whole context of that is where Paul is talking to young Timothy and is saying, "Don't let anyone look down on you because you are young, but set an example for believers in speech, in life, in love, in faith and in purity until I come devote yourself to the public — reading the Scripture, to preaching, to teaching." And then he says to Timothy, "Do not neglect your gift which was given to you through a prophetic message when a body of elders laid their hands on you. Be diligent in these matters, give yourselves wholly to them so that one may see your progress." And then, you know verse 16, when he says, "watch your life and doctrine closely. Persevere in them, because if you do, you'll save both yourself and your hearers." That's a very precious passage to me. Below my name when I'm autographing books, or whatever, I put 1 Timothy 4:16.

CINDEE: Very powerful. Thank you, Hank, so much for setting aside this time to dig into some questions. It's nice to hear from your heart.

HANK: I totally enjoyed having this conversation. I started out trying to get my equilibrium — just did the *Bible Answer Man* broadcast — a little worn out, and you made it fun.

CINDEE: I'm so glad. I know God is with you and is using you to bless so many.

HANK: Well, thank you, Cindee. Say Hi to Rick for me.

SELECTED BIBLIOGRAPHY

"A Brief Chronology of Walter R. Martin's Ministry." *Christian Research Newsletter* 2, no. 4, 1989.

Cindee Martin Morgan. YouTube channel. https://www.youtube.com/channel/UCnqEtvWV90KFQahzoxgdg5A.

The Editors. "What Did the Reformers Think about the Eastern Orthodox Church?" *Christianity Today*, August 8, 2008. https://www.christianitytoday.com/history/2008/august/what-did-reformers-think-about-eastern-orthodox-church.html.

Martin, Walter. *The Kingdom of the Cults*. Minneapolis: Bethany Fellowship, Inc., Publishers, 1972.

Ross, Mark. "In Essentials Unity, In Non-Essentials Liberty, In All Things Charity." Ligonier Ministries. September 9, 2012. https://www.ligonier.org/learn/articles/essentials-unity-non-essentials-liberty-all-things/.

Ryle, J. C. *Practical Religion*. London: Charles Murray, 1900.

——— "The True Church." Virtue Online. https://www.virtueonline.org/true-church-jc-ryle.

Samuels, Allison. "'The Bible Answer Man' Even Had a Posthumous Solution." *The Los Angeles Times*, October 9, 1989. http://articles.latimes.com/1989-10-09/local/me-210_1_bible-answer-man.

Swanson, Dennis M. "Charles H. Spurgeon and the Nation of Israel: A Non-Dispensational Perspective on a Literal National Restoration." The Spurgeon Archive. http://archive.spurgeon.org/misc/eschat2.php.

WalterMartinJude3. YouTube channel. https://www.youtube.com/results?search_query=walter+martin+jude+3.

ABOUT THE AUTHOR

Cindee Martin Morgan is the daughter of the late Dr. Walter Martin, who was the founder and former president of the Christian Research Institute, and the original *Bible Answer Man*. Cindee was briefly on staff at the Christian Research Institute when her father led CRI. Cindee attended Grand Canyon University for two years — studying music, biblical studies, and creative writing — and is continuing her studies. Her first book, a pro-life time-travel novella titled *Rescue Me*, is available on amazon.com. Cindee has also written two powerful pro-life songs, "Who Will Save The Little Ones" and "Fearfully and Wonderfully Made" (available on amazon.com), produced by her husband Rick Morgan. Both compelling songs are heard worldwide on countless venues. Cindee and Rick have four daughters and six grandchildren. They make their home in Cottage Grove, Minnesota.

Made in the USA
Lexington, KY
15 December 2019